# Staying on the Line

# Staying on the Line

## Blue-Collar Women
## in Contemporary Japan

GLENDA S. ROBERTS

University of Hawaii Press / Honolulu

© 1994 University of Hawaii Press
All rights reserved
Printed in the United States of America

94  95  96  97  98  99    5  4  3  2  1


**Library of Congress Cataloging-in-Publication Data**
Roberts, Glenda Susan, 1955–
Staying on the line : blue-collar women in contemporary Japan /
Glenda S. Roberts.
p.    cm.
Includes bibliographical references and index.
ISBN 0–8248–1531–9. — ISBN 0–8248–1579–3 (pbk.)
1.  Women lingerie industry workers—Japan.  2.  Working class
women—Japan.  3.  Women—Employment—Japan.  I.  Title.
HD6073.C62J37    1994
331.4'0952—dc20            93–27346
CIP


University of Hawaii Press books are printed on acid-free
paper and meet the guidelines for permanence and durability
of the Council on Library Resources

Design by Kenneth Miyamoto

*For Julia*

# Contents

# Acknowledgments

THERE ARE many people to whom I owe sincere and warmest thanks for guiding me along the journey which became this book. At Cornell University, I would like to thank Brett de Bary, Carol Greenhouse, and especially Robert J. Smith, for their advice and encouragement. Ken Parker also gave unstintingly of his editorial and computer skills, as well as friendship over many a bowl of popcorn. For assistance in translation problems, my thanks go to Mrs. Kazuko Smith, Yukiko Nagazumi, and Chieko Morrison.

In Japan, I would like to thank Yoneyama Toshinao, my academic advisor, and his administrative assistant, Matsumura Yoshiko, for their time and effort spent in facilitating my research. For assistance in finding a research site and in setting up interviews, I am indebted to Hayashi Hiroko, Saito Hajime, and Inui Shunen. Moreover I am grateful to Fujii Ryuko, Sakurai Minoru, Sawada Michiyo, and Adachi Mariko for sharing ideas and providing helpful information. I also owe special thanks to Fujiwara Seigo, who acquainted me with current topics in Japanese labor law and introduced me to legal experts and others who showed me new perspectives on labor issues.

This project would not have been possible without the cooperation of the management of the corporation I call Azumi. They gave unstintingly of their time, and their efforts to promote my research as well as make me feel welcome are truly appreciated.

Moreover, I am indebted to the Fulbright-Hays Commission for funding my research, and to Cornell University for supporting me while I wrote my dissertation, on which this book is based. I also thank the Population Institute of the East-West Center in Honolulu, which afforded me the time and wherewithal to transform the dissertation into a manuscript during my time there as a post-doctoral fellow in 1990. I am particularly grateful to Linda G. Martin, now at the Rand Corporation.

To the members of the Japan Ethnology Research Circle at the University of Hawaii at Manoa and particularly Takie Lebra, I owe warmest thanks for guidance and suggestions on various drafts of the manuscript. I am also grateful to Patricia Steinhoff and Jane Bachnik for their insightful critiques.

Last, my thanks go to Jim Nickum, for his editing skills and encouragement all along the way.

But it is to the women whose words I convey in these pages that I owe the greatest debt. For their patience with me, their care and concern for me, their time spent in helping me, and their friendship, I thank them most sincerely.

# Introduction

I struggled to fit the lacy garment into its bag. Perhaps it was the wrong size? How was I to fold it so that the bow would be centered, the cups evenly displayed, the straps tucked underneath? To the right and left of me, my coworkers had completed stacks of neatly folded all-in-ones, while I was still on square one. My supervisor approached, looking perplexed, as if to say: "We gave you the job of packaging because it's the easiest to learn. How could you be so clumsy?" Of course she said no such thing, but explained again with great patience how this garment should be folded, where the tags should be placed, how to stack the bags. "Oh—and don't forget to push the counting device after you complete each one. And it should be on the right, like everyone else's, not in front of you."

How ironic that in order to get my Ph.D. I should find myself back in a factory doing the same kind of tedious work I had done one summer as a college student on the assembly line of a G.E. plant. Then, as now, it was the people who made the job bearable, but I worried that at the pace these women worked I might never have the chance to get to know them.

Azumi Textiles (a pseudonym) is a large manufacturer of lingerie and leisure wear, proud of its well-deserved reputation for the excellence of its products and progressive enough to accommodate my request to spend a year working mornings on the shop floor. So, there I was, in the autumn of 1983, stuffing bags, as I started a two-year study of Japanese blue-collar women.

1

Why blue-collar women? Because the women who appear in the literature—from Rohlen's *For Harmony and Strength* (1974) to Mclendon's "The Office: Way Station or Blind Alley?" (Plath 1983)—are usually the young office girls whose employment is little more than a transition between graduation from school and marriage. Work for them may serve primarily as a dating service, a chance to socialize, a way of funding high-fashion shopping, and a means of saving up a nest egg before "retiring" early for their true vocations as *ryōsai kenbo,* good wives and wise mothers.[1]

But what about the large group of less-well-educated women who have to work on factory floors? Blue-collar women have been the mainstay of light manufacturing industries in Japan since the heyday of the spinning mills at the beginning of the century, yet we have little in-depth information about their lives. Indeed, in 1985, 25 percent of Japanese women workers were employed in the manufacturing sector (OECD 1987). What are the women who choose to keep their jobs throughout marriage and the childbearing years until they reach retirement age like? What is their work ethic, what are their goals, and how are these mediated by their roles as wives and mothers? These questions had not been pursued. I sought the answers through my interactions and interviews with women factory workers at Azumi, as well as in a subsequent year of literature review and interviewing of women workers in other industrial settings.

Azumi, like most Japanese companies, agrees with society that women's primary role in life is as full-time wife and mother. It manifests this through gender stratification in hiring, placement, promotion, and retirement. Yet the majority of the women with whom I worked said they wanted to continue through to retirement, or at least as long as they were physically able. They recognized the difficulties involved, especially given the company's attitude, but they were tenacious. Why? Because, to them, a woman's domestic role is not only as wife and mother but also as household manager. They work to bring in income, which is all the more necessary given the expense of raising children "properly" in contemporary Japan. The women with whom I worked had not sought employment out of a desire for autonomy. Their participation in the work force was a broadening of the concept of the homemaker's role rather than a rejection of or emancipation from it.

My research comes at a time when, nationwide, increasing numbers of women are staying in the work force beyond the culturally accepted "retirement" signpost for women, which is marriage. Those who do "retire" at marriage are reentering the work force when their children reach school age, or even before. They are changing the shape of women's paid employment to an M-curve where the valley of the M is increasingly less pronounced and the second peak of the M is increasingly high. (See Chapter 1 for further discussion of the M-curve.) While this study was under way, changes in the Civil Code and Labor Standards Act were also being formulated at the national level, to bring Japan's laws into line with the United Nations Convention on the Elimination of All Forms of Discrimination against Women, which Japan had signed in 1980. The Equal Opportunity in Employment Act (EEOA) was enacted in 1985 and promulgated in 1986. I will discuss the EEOA at greater length in the Conclusion. Here, however, I wish to emphasize that the issue of women's increasing presence in paid employment and their treatment in the work force were of considerable concern, at both the national level and the level of the firm, at the time of the study. At the individual level among my coworkers, it was not so much debated as lived, with all the inherent struggles and contradictions. From the lives of my coworkers emerges a portrait of what it is like to be a woman in the "system" of lifetime employment, seniority wages, and the enterprise union.

From Azumi's regular-status male employees, as for men in other large firms, total commitment to the firm is expected, taken for granted. Furthermore, a man's commitment to his firm also signifies and stands as a measure of his commitment to his family: the harder he works for the firm, the higher he climbs, the greater are his household's income and social status. His worth as a man is not measured by how well he keeps his household or how able his children are. For a married woman, on the other hand, this is hardly further from the truth. Inasmuch as she is a regular employee, she must work hard for the firm; but the more commitment she demonstrates, the more subject she is to criticism vis-à-vis her role as housewife/mother, and the more difficult it becomes to manage the dual roles. Azumi's women worked overtime within the limits allowed them under the Labor Standards Act, and they often refrained from taking their vacation time in order to keep production running smoothly. However, while they wanted their regular-status, "lifetime employment" jobs, they did not want to commit themselves to their firms to the exclusion of their families.

Women's desire to contribute to the household income is nothing new. What is new is a shift in the locus of work for urban housewives from in-home piecework *(naishoku)* to work outside as *paato,* or employees of nonregular status.[2] That jobs are important to many women workers—not only to regular employees such as those I knew at Azumi but also to *paato*—was obvious from the many interviews I conducted with *paato* in various manufacturing industries. This topic merits a book in itself, however, and as Azumi hired only a small number of *paato,* I shall not deal with them here.

Shinotsuka (1983) points out that some have mistakenly identified this externalization of work for women as a new social problem, betokening the breakdown of the family. In fact, however, women who leave home to work are far from a "new breed" of individualistic, "me-first" women who neglect their families. Nor are they shirkers at work. They recognize, and for the most part approve of, the system's standards and are doing their best to conform to them within the limits set by their duties at home. When the demands of home and family or health begin to exceed the point where the pace and quality of work can be maintained, they often step down from supervisory positions or quit their jobs. Compromising the work ethic is not an option that these women could or would choose.

This volume focuses on the tensions between women who want to work until retirement and the cultural view of women that regards them primarily as mothers. The women themselves adhere to these cultural definitions of womanhood. Yet they also persist in trying to maintain careers until retirement, against considerable odds. "Staying on the line" as regular employees until retirement certainly means bucking the company's plan, and in many cases it also entails going against the wishes of their families.

## Methodology

As an anthropologist, I felt that my questions could best be answered by a long-term participant-observation study of one setting, supplemented by interviews with my coworkers, as well as with a number of women workers in other blue-collar industries. For my purposes I needed a work setting where there was a sizable proportion of women workers of varying age and marital status, in both regular and part-time employment.

I was looking at questions of attitudes toward women's role as worker and wife/mother rather than at the ways in which particular industries might vary in their treatment of women workers, so I did not specify a type of manufacturer. Contacts in Japan were negotiating for me at three different urban locations, all in the Kansai (western Japan) region—a confectionery shop, a shoe and rubber products factory, and a lingerie factory. In the end, the confectionery and shoe factory rejected the proposal, citing economic downturn. The lingerie manufacturer, Azumi, agreed.

Azumi's president was proud of his company and its success, and welcomed the study. Actually, one of my Japanese mentors cautioned me that conditions at Azumi were likely to be much better than at most places, so I should take care to interview women at other factories and to be aware of national statistics on women workers' attitudes, their conditions and treatment.

What were the opinions of Azumi's male employees on the matters at hand? As a consequence of the site being an apparel factory, there were only two men among 242 workers who were engaged in any capacity similar in job content and status to that of my women co-workers: one worked at a pressing machine in the fabric-cutting section and the other shipped boxes. Both were middle-aged employees who had had diverse careers before coming to work at Azumi, and I had numerous conversations with them. Their viewpoints enriched my knowledge of Azumi a great deal.

Most men enter more generalized management-track jobs with career possibilities that necessitate a willingness to accept transfer to any of the company's branch factories or offices. A young man repairing sewing machines or hefting boxes this year may well find himself transferred to the accounting department of the main office the following year. This would be extremely rare for a woman. Aside from conversations I had while teaching English to a group of young men at headquarters, my contact with such male employees was minimal. I did, however, interview six men in management positions and a male union official, to learn their views of the women they supervised. I had little opportunity to socialize with male employees on a regular basis, since our paths so seldom crossed. Women worked together, played together, and ate together. Efforts to create a new pattern that included socializing with the men invited gossip.

At the Azumi factory, hiring and placement were quite sex-segregated, with women usually entering dead-end jobs of cutting, sewing, inspection, and packaging. There were also a few jobs at the factory office for female high-school graduates. At Azumi's shipping center, women were mainly engaged in inspection, packaging, and office work. When I left, management was starting to move women into the loading and shipping of boxes as well, in an effort to "rationalize" the work force. The main office hired female designers as well as office workers: the few women who were promoted beyond the subsection-chief level came from these ranks. Azumi Corporation also hired a large contingent of salesladies for their retail shops, but I had no contact with these women.

On my first day, the head of the factory introduced me to my work group. He explained that I was a student at one of the local universities who had an interest in learning about women in the work force in Japan, so I wanted some practical experience to go along with my studies. Hence I would be a part-time worker with them for the coming year. He asked them for their cooperation, and so did I. Thus began my career as an Azumi *paato*. Although everyone knew about my research topic, most people soon became accustomed to the idea, or they forgot about it. Gradually I realized that most took me for a student who needed the extra income. They were curious about me as a foreigner, as a woman, as a daughter, and as a wife. To them, my academic role was—well—academic.

After I had settled down to a routine, I began to see the problems of straddling the fence. How much should I associate with management at the main office? How open should I be with my coworkers about my activities there? As I was only working half-days at the factory, Azumi headquarters had offered me a desk in the Health Management Office, if I cared to study there in the afternoons. At first, as a response to this gesture of goodwill and for convenience, I accepted the offer. It was especially helpful on those days when I taught English to a group of young executives there, a service which the company had requested.

Yet, before long, I felt I had to limit these contacts with headquarters, as my coworkers always wanted to know where I was going and why. Contacts with headquarters seemed to create distance between us. There was a definite hierarchy in status, with the factory ranking below the main office. Unlike my coworkers, I was hired by the main office and, as the only foreign researcher, could easily obtain access to people in upper management who were no more than figures on a stage to them.

To minimize this distance-putting, I played down my relationships with headquarters and did not actively foster new ones. If I had spent more time creating smooth personal relationships with those who controlled access to information on personnel policies and the salary and benefits structure, I could present Azumi as an institution. However, it would undoubtedly have been at the cost of access to my coworkers and their families, who are, after all, the main subject of this study.

Interviews, which I began conducting in January of 1984, informal conversations with workers, and my own observations form the basis of my research. Interviews consisted of a set of open-ended questions (see Appendix). Of the eighteen women in the factory Inspection and Packaging section (hereafter I&P), fifteen agreed to be interviewed. Other women interviewed were friends of my coworkers who worked in other sections and women in the shipping center (see Table 1).

I also interviewed the only male employee of the factory I&P, nurses in the Health Section of the main office, the union secretary, and the section chief of the I&P Shipping Center.

I feel extremely grateful that I was allowed to do this study at Azumi. Although my findings may not always reflect favorably on the company, Azumi's treatment of women workers is in no way unusual. Its position reflects a deeply rooted ideology in Japan that sees men and women in complementary but distinct spheres of action in society. Men work outside the home; women maintain the household. The reality, however, is that women have become an increasingly significant part of the nonfamily work force in the past fifteen years. The conflict between this exigency and the company's vision for its women employees was a source of individual frustration but not group action. Indeed, many women sympathized with the company's viewpoint. My coworkers did not see themselves as wave-makers or as feminists, but as women who needed incomes and were determined to make them. Surely we can see them as activists, however, in their very tenacity in the face of pressure to quit. Perhaps they were not sign-wavers or group-organizers, but they voted with their feet—every day, through the factory doors in the morning and back out the doors in the evening. By their willpower to remain on the job, these women and others like them are gradually changing the shape of Japanese society.

I, as a Western "career woman," was glad to have the option of bowing out of my *paato* status at the end of one year's employment and retreating to a world that offers more alternatives. What I would have desired for my coworkers was not always what they got nor nec-

## Table 1. Interview Respondents

| Name | Age | Years of Service | Education | Employee Status | Marital Status | No. of Children |
|---|---|---|---|---|---|---|
| Fujii, N. | 28 | 13 | JH | Reg | M | 2+ |
| Hanami, R. | 30 | 12 | HS | Reg | M | 0 |
| Hasegawa, S. | 52 | 10 | PWE* | Reg | M | 2 |
| Irahara, S. | 24 | 9 | HS | Reg, ex-shisutaa | S | 0 |
| Kamida, T. | 37 | 22 | JH | Reg, Hanchō | M | 2 |
| Koga, M. | 30 | 15 | JH | Reg | M | 2 |
| Kushida, K. | 46 | 10 | HS | *Paato* | M | 2 |
| Matsumura, A. | 36 | 15 | HS | Reg, Hanchō | S | 0 |
| Mihata, S. | 48 | 7 | HS | *Paato* | M | 2 |
| Murakami, K. | 40 | 25 | JH | Reg, Kakarichō | S | 0 |
| Murata, H. | 23 | 8 | JH | Reg | S | 0 |
| Nakada, C. | 43 | 14 | HS | Reg | W | 1 |
| Nakanishi, M. | 52 | 8 | JH | Reg | M | 2 |
| Nishitani, H. | 32 | 16 | HS | Reg | M | 2+ |
| Ogawa, S. | 43 | 10 | HS | Reg | M | 2 |
| Ota, M. | 40 | 25 | JH | Reg, ex-shisutaa | M | 2 |
| Shimizu, Y. | 32 | 17 | JH | Reg | M | 2 |
| Tahara, J. | 53 | 25 | PWE | ex-*kakarichō*, Shokutaku | D | 1 |
| Taniguchi, N. | 48 | 7 | JH | Reg | S | 0 |
| Usui, T. | 31 | 16 | JH | Reg, ex-Hanchō | M | 2 |
| Yamamoto, M. | 22 | 7 | JH | Reg | S | 0 |

*PWE = prewar elementary school

essarily what most of them desired for themselves. As an anthropologist, however, I have tried to present Japanese working women's lives in their own cultural context. I do not want to make the women seem to be feminists when they were not, but I do not want to give the impression that they were perfectly content with the status quo either.

What was that status quo? Let us turn to the shop floor for an overview.

## Azumi: The Context

Azumi was different from many manufacturers in that most of its women were regular, not *paato*, employees. Most other manufacturers experienced an economic decline after the oil shock of 1973–1974, leading them to "rationalize" their work forces through such practices as lessening the number of recruits taken on each year, encouragement of early retirement, and the hiring of *paato* workers, largely housewives whose household budgets were feeling the pinch (Fuse 1982; Shinotsuka 1983). In contrast, Azumi grew steadily in the 1970s, and it was not until the early 1980s that it began to notice a downturn. It was at this point that Azumi started its own rationalization drive, greatly reducing the scale of the "main-office" factory (which had been its first), ceasing to hire new blue-collar workers, and shifting workers to jobs at another location. It had already established subsidiaries in rural areas of Japan and in other parts of Asia where costs were much less than in the urban setting where I worked.

In 1983 when I entered Azumi I found, to my surprise, that my immediate work group consisted mostly of married women with long years of service to the company. Some of them had started after junior high school or high school and stayed through marriage and pregnancies. Others entered after their children were school-age, but they had entered as regular employees because the company was expanding and needed regulars. Whatever the case, the women felt lucky to have jobs as regulars when most women of their age could only find jobs as *paato*. They shared the desire to keep their jobs. One of my coworkers described our work group as the "survivors," those who had stuck it out through years of being under the thumb of a tough boss, standing firm regardless of their husbands' disapproval of their working or the company's hints that perhaps they were getting too old for the work. Thus, my sample, mostly married blue-collar women working as regular employees for a major corporation, is not the norm. From them, though, I learned the reasons why lifetime employment as a full-fledged "regular" employee is difficult for a blue-collar woman worker.

Nationwide, Azumi had roughly four thousand employees, nearly three-fourths of them women. When I began the study, 49.9 percent of Azumi's female work force consisted of salesladies. Office workers were next at 34 percent, with factory workers following at 13.5 percent. Designers were the fewest at 2.5 percent. Azumi had increased its female work force by about one-third from 1974 through 1985. The percentages of women employed in the various job categories, however, fluctuated a great deal in accordance with company policies to streamline operations, increase the sales force[3] and shift the bulk of the manufacturing work to rural and overseas subsidiaries (see Table 2).

How representative of Japanese women workers were Azumi's women in terms of years of service to the company? Overall, the average in 1985 was 7.2 years, slightly more than the national average of 6.5 years but still far below the male average of 11.6 years. Yet, if we look at years of service by job category, the difference in length of service is quite remarkable, with factory workers and designers far outlasting office workers and salesladies. Moreover, although years of service increased steadily for all categories of Azumi's women workers from 1974 to 1985, the trend is especially pronounced for factory workers and designers (see Table 3).

Table 2. Occupational Distribution of Azumi's Female Work Force, 1974–1985 (Percent)

|  | 1974 | 1980 | 1984 | 1985 |
|---|---|---|---|---|
| Blue-collar | 34.9 | 20.7 | 11.2 | 8.9 |
| Designers | 4.4 | 3.0 | 2.4 | 2.2 |
| Office workers | 25.1 | 32.9 | 34.2 | 35.2 |
| Salesladies | 35.6 | 43.5 | 52.3 | 53.8 |

Table 3. Azumi's Female Labor Force by Occupation and Years of Service, 1974–1985 (Percent)

|  | 1974 | 1980 | 1983 | 1985 |
|---|---|---|---|---|
| Blue-collar | 4.7 | 6.3 | 7.9 | 10.1 |
| Designers | 4.5 | 7.4 | 9.1 | 10.0 |
| Salesladies | 3.2 | 3.1 | 3.4 | 3.6 |
| Office workers | 4.1 | 4.2 | 4.8 | 5.2 |

Why should this be so? The principal factor is probably the absence of new recruitment. When the company began cutting back on output at the main office factory and ceased hiring new factory workers there, those who were left were the "survivors." Many of my coworkers entered as new junior-high-school graduates in the late sixties, and others were hired as mid-career entrants during the mid-seventies when Azumi's factory operation was going strong. They stayed through the following decade as new recruiting dropped drastically at this location. One reason they chose to stay on was economic. In the case of the small number of designers at Azumi, the company may have had a positive attitude toward their retention, as their skills are hard to replace without extensive training.

The salesladies were in a different situation. They were hired straight out of high school and were expected to quit at marriage. The subdepartment head of personnel, a man, explicitly stated it would be not only costly to have such low-skilled employees stay on, but also would damage the company image. Azumi wanted young women selling their products, not aging matrons in their late twenties and thirties. This expectation probably accounts for the low average years of service among salesladies, although additional factors such as inconvenient working conditions may play a role.

As I mentioned earlier, nationwide the percentage of married women employees (nonagricultural) has increased steadily in the last decade, from 51.3 percent of the female work force in 1975 to 58.8 percent in 1985. If we include those who are divorced or widowed, the figures are 62.1 percent and 68.2 percent, respectively (Rodosho Fujinkyoku 1987:16). Azumi has shown a similar trend, going from 16.3 percent in 1974 to 18.6 percent in 1984. In Azumi's case, these figures are skewed downward by the large proportion of salesladies. If we exclude them from the calculations, the percentage of married women went up from 25.4 percent in 1974 to 39 percent in 1984. At the main office factory, 48 percent of the women were married. By comparison, 81 percent of Azumi's male employees were married.

As of March 1, 1984, there were 242 employees in the main office factory: 18 men, 224 women. Of the women, 49 percent were married. The average age of the women was 29.65; of the men, 39.06. All the women were regular employees, except for eight *paato*. The average length of their service was 10.11 years; of the men's, 11.16. (This is long in comparison with nationwide statistics for average years of service for women, which was 6.5 years in 1984.) Following is a list of terms I will use frequently in the text. Worker classification is in ascending order.

*paato:* A nonregular employee who works about one hour less per day than regular employees. She is paid hourly wages, and her benefits are few. She is on a short-term contract usually renewed perfunctorily. *Paato* are not allowed to join the union.

*shokutaku:* An employee whose status is between that of *paato* and *shain.* Her benefits are greater than those of *paato* but less than those of regular employees. In many firms, employees (usually male) are kept on after retirement as *shokutaku* in unranked jobs at fractions of their former salaries.

*shain:* A regular employee and union member until one reaches the *kachō* class.

*shisutaa:* Lit. "sister." The lowest supervisory rank in the factory.

*hanchō:* The leader of a *han,* or group of about twenty or more workers.

*insutorakutaa:* Lit. "instructor." An employee (female) highly skilled in sewing who teaches sewing skills.

*kakarichō:* Subsection chief.

*kachō:* Section chief.

*fukubuchō:* Subdepartment head.

*buchō:* Department head.

*kōjōchō:* Factory head.

*shachō:* President.

In the Inspection and Packaging Section where I worked as a packager, there were nineteen people: eighteen women and one man. Ten of the women were married, one widowed, and seven unmarried. Of the married and widowed women, all but one had children. Two of the women were *paato.* The *kakarichō* (subsection chief) oversaw the operations of the entire section. The subsection chief was a woman, Murakami san, unusual in this company. There was no section chief for the I&P; Murakami san reported directly to the factory manager. Jobs in the section were packaging, labeling, and inspection of garments. Four of us were assigned to packaging and labeling, one (the male) to shipping, eleven to inspection, one to office work, and two to facilitation of the work flow. Those two held the lowest supervisory rank, that of *shisutaa* (from the English word "sister"). Management assigned the term *shisutaa* to these work facilitators in the 1960s when there were many young recruits who needed a little extra "sisterly" supervision and advice. Each *shisutaa* had many charges at a time and was enjoined to keep them in line. Unlike the case of informal senior/junior relationships in which, as Rohlen (1974) describes, seniors foster a young male employee's path upward, *shisutaa* did not have the ability to affect the promotion of their female charges or to negotiate or bargain with the *hanchō* (group leader) or any higher supervisor on their behalf.

Packagers stood behind tables, with an item counter and a pile of garments before them. A packager would first check through the pile to be certain each item was of the same style and size, then take the top item, spread it out on the table, and fold it in a set fashion, checking to ensure that the proper tags were in place. She would then insert it into a vinyl case that had been prepared previously with a colored cardboard insert stating the style, color, size, and special features of the garment. After this she pushed the counter and stacked the finished packages so that the shipper could box them. She had to take great care that each was folded to fit neatly inside the case. Depending on the fabric and size of the garment, this could be difficult. Packagers also made boxes and stamped inserts, and did spot-check inspections of garments previously passed by the regular inspectors.

Labelers sewed tags onto garments, stamped inserts, and made boxes. They also packaged and did spot-check inspections.

Inspectors worked while standing behind long tables, garments to be inspected piled before them. An inspector would first check to make sure that each garment in the pile had the same size and style number. She then picked up each item, looking at it carefully in a precise, set order as she pulled and stretched the garment through her hands. She would look for defects in the fabric, irregular stitching or missed stitches, twisted straps, missing ornamentation, rips, dirt, discoloration, uncut threads, and so on. The more ornate the product, the more difficult it was to inspect. Black thread on a black item was particularly hard to see.

The workday was from 8:30 to 5:10, with a forty-five minute lunch break and a fifteen-minute break at 3:00 P.M. The morning began with a bell at 8:20 to signal that we should get to our stations. By this time most people had changed into their workshop shoes and the company jacket. At the 8:30 bell we would form a circle and greet each other. Production targets were announced, and the *kakarichō* would acknowledge those who had reached their targets the previous day. The factory manager often came to the morning ceremony to lecture us on the economic condition of the company, new policies, new product lines or business ventures, and so on. He occasionally simply told a humorous story or cracked a joke, but the content of his talks was usually serious. People listened attentively.

The pace of the day was brisk and the work atmosphere stern, in part due to our *kakarichō*. She did not allow us to chat, chew gum, hum, or whistle, on the ground that such conduct would impede our concentration. Breaks ended at the bell, and people would begin to get back to their stations before it rang. Indeed, sometimes employees worked through portions of their breaks. There was no loitering in the halls or restrooms. Some people would linger to chat in the cafeteria after lunch, but most would bring their snacks upstairs to the break areas of each section and converse there. For most of my year at Azumi, I worked mornings (I started out working afternoons, arriving after lunch, but after a few weeks of this switched to mornings.) I soon discovered that if I wanted to become at all familiar with my coworkers, I would have to arrive early for the prework snack that some chose to eat together and stay through lunch until the 12:40 P.M. bell rang to signal the impending end of the lunch break.

At 5:10 the dismissal bell rang, but only the *paato* were free to leave. The regular employees remained for an extra ten minutes to clean the shop. That done, we formed a circle and were dismissed. If there was no overtime, most workers would then rush downstairs to the locker room to change into street attire and hurry to catch the train or ride their bicycles home.

In April of 1984 the company decided to dissolve the factory's Inspection and Packaging Section and transfer most of its workers to the shipping center, to do similar jobs. This afforded me the opportunity to experience a different setting: the new I&P Division was over three times the size of the factory's section, once we were included. It was headed by a male *kachō*, one male *kakarichō*, two female *hanchō* (supervisors of groups of about thirty employees), and four *shisutaa*. The work was the same but the methods were different. We worked in groups and were given group rather than the individual targets we had at the factory. Moreover, the new methods of inspection and packaging we had to learn were sometimes contrary to those we had been taught at the factory. As the *kachō* said, we were like *oyome* (brides) who had to learn the ways of our new home.

Many factors combined to make our transition relatively easy. In particular, the work atmosphere was much more relaxed. We were allowed to chat and joke a bit, and could even remove our uniform jackets if we felt hot. We were also free to wear street shoes. We did not run to and from the restrooms and could even take a minute now and then for a cup of green tea to quench our thirst. Topics at morning circle tended to be lighter. Doi *kachō* once read us a good recipe, and another time he discoursed on the bad effects of high-heeled shoes on posture. Moreover, workers took turns leading the morning ceremony, reading the slogan of the day (see Azumi's Ten "Fight" Slogans, at the end of this chapter) and giving a speech on some newsworthy topic. Subjects ranged from remedies for illnesses to good wishes for the season to the individual's concern over social problems or even family matters.

At least once a month we were called downstairs for a joint morning ceremony with all the other divisions in the center. At this time the department head would speak or we would have visitors from the main office. Topics were usually more "serious," concerned with production and company goals. At these times quality control groups might also give presentations on how they had managed to implement new techniques to improve efficiency.

The buildings of the shipping center were newer, the facilities more modern, the workplace brighter. The cafeteria had a large color television set, which employees watched during breaks and which doubled as a video screen when we watched speeches of the president of Azumi Corporation.

The *kachō* told me that the factory was harsher because it was at the center of the production process. I would add that the more relaxed atmosphere of the shipping center was in part due to the magnanimity of the *kachō* himself. Coming from the factory, my coworkers and I thought life was pleasant at the shipping center. Some of the old hands from the I&P were more likely to be critical, as they had been trained the hard way, but they were relieved to have made the transition at all.

This portrait of blue-collar women holds some surprises for those who have considered the system from the viewpoint of the male employee. Here let me offer a preview of the ensuing chapters. Chapter 1 discusses male and female gender roles in Japan and how the perceptions of gender contribute to shaping women's career trajectories nationally and at Azumi.

Chapter 2 discusses the challenge of work on the shop floor and examines the strategies my coworkers used to meet the challenge. The consequences of failure are also discussed.

The challenge of a lifetime of line work with few opportunities for job training or rotation is the subject of Chapter 3.

In Chapter 4, I take up a question that is frequently asked but not often answered: why don't Japanese workers use their allotted vacation time? This chapter details the dynamics of asking for time off and the hurdles of getting it. In the process I show how my coworkers juggle the competing demands of home and work, and how their husbands sometimes step in to help.

Women who have worked ten or twenty years in the company, whether they are high-flyers or plodders, are veterans in every sense of the word. The career trajectories of four women, including their perspectives on promotion and getting into supervisory positions, is the topic of Chapter 5.

The value of men's after-hours socializing to the harmony of the workplace is well known. How about women? Their constraints, from their family responsibilities to negative cultural perceptions of women, shape how they relate to each other, on and off the job. This is the subject of Chapter 6.

Chapter 7 discusses the channels women use—or do not use—to air their complaints, from the labor union to the health staff to friends and family. Although much is said about interdependence in Japanese society, women workers have difficulty improving their workplaces because they do not see themselves as interdependent. As Pharr (1991) found in her study of the "tea pourer's rebellion," solidarity among women workers is not easily built. This chapter explores the reasons why.

A book about women workers would hardly be complete without a discussion of strategies for child care, which in Japanese society is felt to be largely the responsibility of mothers. In a society where there is thought to be no replacement for a mother's care, what do women workers with small children do? Chapter 8 outlines day-care options and coping strategies of my coworkers. I also discuss another responsibility of married women, household budgeting, as well as my coworkers' attitudes toward spending.

By and large, Japanese men are able to meet the demands of their work because they have professional housewives at home running family life for them. When one's wife, too, has a job as a regular employee, however, life becomes much more complicated. Many of my coworkers' husbands did not want them to work, yet they worked anyway. Chapter 9 tells the story of the emotional and physical support women do or do not get from their spouses and children, and shows how support is sometimes negotiated over the years.

This, then, was where I found myself in the fall of 1983. As I wended my way through the layers of Azumi's system, I began to see that married women, not through protest but by their very presence as regular employees, were challenging, even redefining, the tenets of an ideology that permeates Japanese society—that of good wife, wise mother.

## *Azumi's Ten "Fight" Slogans*

1. Work is not something one is given; it is something one should make for oneself.

2. Work is not something one receives passively, but is something on which one moves, seizing the initiative.

3. Do not think of the dimensions of your work; always throw your whole strength into it.

4. Keep aiming at work you think difficult; you have made progress when you accomplish it.

5. Do not fear friction [in personal relationships] but keep improving yourself. People are inclined to inertia.

6. Be a leader. There is a great difference in the long run between those who lead and those who follow.

7. If you have a plan and hold it for a long time, patience, inventiveness, genuine effort, and hope will be born of it.

8. If you lack self-confidence, your work contains neither force nor perseverance nor even substance.

9. Service is the kind of thing that allows not a second of rest; one must always be fully on the alert in every respect.

10. Do not worry about being wise or foolish. Arrogance will not change one's value. Just perform. Otherwise you will be regretful and lack moral courage.

**DATE DUE**

# 1

# Azumi's Good Wives and Wise Mothers

AZUMI'S PRODUCTION work force was made up almost totally of women. Most of the garments they sewed, inspected, and packaged were targeted for the female market, to "make women beautiful." What was the company president's philosophy on gender roles, I wondered. Was he proud of his work force? Did he encourage them in their efforts to make Azumi known for its quality worldwide? One day, in the employee lunchroom, the answer fell into my lap.

On an anniversary of the founding of the company, the company president prepared a speech for all the company employees to watch on video during lunch break. In the speech he took us from his wartime experiences to the postwar devastation. He then discussed the enormous energy that had been poured into rebuilding Japan. What I found interesting was that he used this occasion to lecture his employees on the perils of following modern trends in changing male and female roles. According to him, it was the strength of traditional Japanese women that was behind Japan's economic recovery. These women presumably were not leaving their children in day-care centers to go out to work, but were professional housewives, maintaining the home and keeping their husbands on the right track. In his opinion, today's breakdown in the separation of spheres will lead to social chaos. Men, who used to be kept in line by their wives, now have no one to guide and encourage them, no one to counterbalance their excesses. In his metaphor, the puppeteers, lured by the glitter of the stage, have abandoned their puppets to become actresses themselves.

Yet without the puppeteers, the puppets have no strength, no life. And this, he says, bodes ill for Japan's future. In his words:

> Thinking of Japan's past, when we ask who was greater, men or women, it is true that it was the men who were in the foreground, engaged in activities such as politics, economics, and education. But in the background, there were always the women, who, with firm hand, maintained the household and brought up the children, encouraging their husbands and sharing their hardships. One could say that men were like the puppets in *bunraku* [Japanese traditional puppet theatre], always on center stage, but there is someone who makes the puppets dance. In Japan, the men were the puppets who were made to dance, and in the shadows were the wonderful, staunch women. I can reach no other conclusion. The postwar recovery, which required tremendous strength, is also due to such women.
>
> When I came to this realization, however, I was struck with fear. Nowadays, women have totally changed. The women who had had a wonderful tradition and extraordinary strength have now begun to fall. [Long pause.] Formerly, men worked but also played, and were unfaithful as well. They did both good and bad things. And women had accepted that, firmly maintaining the household. But now [lowers voice], women have begun to change greatly. They no longer maintain the household. They dislike raising children. That is what it has come to. And women, just like men, or, perhaps more so, have become lost in amusements. Today, who is going to maintain the household? I think that Japan has already started on the road to ruin, since so few people are alert to this. Unless women awaken, and take hold of themselves, more and more good women will be made fools by these new social trends. When modern trends advance, and women start having affairs and such while their husbands are at work, what will become of this wonderful Japan with her traditions which have continued for over two thousand years, and which led her to become this extraordinary economic superpower?
>
> Azumi was founded with the grand purpose of making women beautiful. But beauty is not only a matter of form. A splendid heart and a beautiful spirit are even more important. I want to make this anniversary an occasion to instill this kind of thinking

firmly into the women of Azumi. [In the past], as fitting comple-
ments to such splendid women, there were great men. However,
when the women changed the men began to fall as well. Men no
longer have strength. There are few manly men nowadays. And I
feel that this is a result of this kind of [modern] women. Well, in
this way men and women have passed forty years since the war. I
think that we have reached the age when each of us as individuals,
for the sake of our grandchildren, must seriously consider what
Japan should be like in the twenty-first century.

We can confidently assume that the company president approves of
the traditional separation of male and female spheres of influence. His
philosophy would encourage the practice of women retiring from the
work force upon marriage and condemn those who did not. My coworkers did not seem surprised to hear his views. They continued eating their lunch, and after the video was over they picked up their conversations where they had left off. These women, who had spent many
years at Azumi, were quite aware of the president's philosophy, for it
was evident in the gender stratification of the workplace. Moreover,
his are culturally acceptable, mainstream values. He might sound old-
fashioned to some in Japan, but views like his continue to provide the
ideological underpinnings of employment practices, and the worries
he expressed are shared by many, women and men alike.

Most of my coworkers' husbands were regular employees in local
factories or small businesses, or they worked for Azumi. Until the mid
1970s, most urban women married to salaried employees did not have
jobs outside the home. Had my coworkers planned to work after marriage, and if not, what made them change their minds? Had they for-
saken the traditional role of *ryōsai kenbo* (good wife, wise mother) as
Azumi's president so feared, or was this new pattern a different interpretation of it?

## The Professional Housewife Model

In the literature on middle-class families of college-educated men and
their junior-college-educated, ex-office lady (OL) wives, we find that
Japanese women are socialized to become wives and mothers, or, as
Suzanne Vogel put it, "professional housewives." Men are socialized
to become *daikoku bashira*, the financial pillars of their households.

Vogel (1978), Edwards (1989), and others analyze this relationship as interdependent, mutually sustaining. Each role set is fixed, allowing very little overlap. By acting her or his role set, however, the individual commands power and respect. According to many researchers, Japanese professional housewives assume an authority greater than that of their Western counterparts: they alone manage the family budget, make major purchases, dole out allowances to their spouses, decide where the children are to be sent to school, supervise homework, and so on. They also take on most of the nurturing tasks that go into raising a family, forming close bonds of dependency with their children as well as becoming motherly caretakers of their husbands, anticipating the unspoken needs of all family members (Lebra 1976; Salamon 1975). Although one might think that the domestically oriented wife and her public-domain-oriented husband are "traditional" gender configurations in Japan, this is not so. The prominence of the professional housewife role is a relatively recent, postwar phenomenon, accompanying the shift from primary- to secondary-sector employment. From the late nineteenth century, it was common for young unmarried women to leave their rural homes for a stint in the spinning mills before marriage. In farms and family businesses, where workplace and household are not separate (and the economic activity is interwoven with household identity), mill girls and farm girls became wives who participated actively in the economic activity of the household. As men who had been farmers migrated to the cities to work in factories and offices, however, their wives, who previously had fulfilled active roles in agriculture, now devoted themselves to the domestic domain. If a man did not earn enough to meet the family's needs, it was common for his wife to take in piecework *(naishoku)* from local factories. Married women with able, employed husbands were not expected to work outside the home.

During this transitional period the ideology of *ryōsai kenbo* developed and became widespread. By the time Ezra Vogel did his study of Japan's middle class in 1963, the ideology was well entrenched. Today, too, it thrives, at least in the better-educated, well-off households of Imamura's 1987 study. It is questionable to what extent this ideology is embraced by less-well-educated people in blue- and pink-collar occupations. Even if they do not hold it as ideal, however, it certainly affects their lives, since the people owning and managing the factories and businesses do.

## *Employment and* Ryōsai Kenbo

How does the ideology of the professional housewife influence women's choices in the labor market? In the *ryōsai kenbo* model, trying to "have it all," a family and a career of her own, is definitely beyond the bounds of a woman's role set. Instead, she is encouraged to work until marriage, then quit to raise a family and reenter the labor force, if at all, after the children are grown. The resulting pattern of employment is known as the "M-curve," where the rate of employment declines between the ages of twenty-four and thirty-four. (NIEVR 1988; see Figure 1).

Until the first peak is reached in the mid-twenties at 65.2 percent, women's participation in the paid employment sector is considered normal and is encouraged socially as well as economically. During this period, a woman's desire to work is most congruent with ideological assumptions about her role. The downward trend begins in the age range 25–29, with a 22 percent drop, and reaches its lowest point at ages 30–34, dropping 9 percent more. This represents the period of greatest conflict between women's continued employment and their roles as wives and mothers. Role contradictions notwithstanding, 33.8 percent of women are employees during this period of the life cycle, in the "trough" of the M. Granted, some of them are single women, widows, or divorcées for whom the continuation of work poses less of a cultural dilemma. However, many of these female employees are married and have young children. My research focuses on this age group of paid employees, the one that faces the most severe role contradictions. What the M-curve fails to show us is how many are working as full-time, regular employees. Many may be temporary workers, dispatch workers, or *paato*.

Although the professional housewife model for women is still very much in evidence today, changes in the economy and society are bringing about modifications in women's response to it. A 1985 report published by the Women's Bureau of the Ministry of Labor notes that salary increases have not kept pace with rises in the price of housing and education. These factors lead women to seek extradomestic employment even after they have families. With the post-oil-shock restructuring of the workplace, they have the opportunity to do so. Reluctant to add to their tenured work force, employers created *paato* jobs in large numbers. As a result, women are working as (nonfamily)

Figure 1. Women's Working Status and Desire to Work

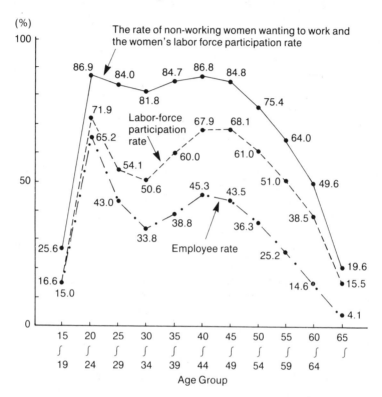

*Source:* The labor force participation rate and employee rate are based on the "Labor Force Survey" (1985) by The Statistics Department of the Management and Coordination Agency; the rate of non-working women wanting to work is based on the "Employment Status Survey" (1982) by The Statistics Bureau of the Management and Coordination Agency. Reprinted in National Institute of Employment and Vocational Research, ed., *Women Workers in Japan* (1988), p. 26.

employees in record numbers. In 1975 women employees (nonagricultural, nonfamily workers) comprised 59.8 percent of all women workers; by 1985 they comprised 68.2 percent. Takenaka (1987) notes that the gains are due mostly to married, middle-aged women reentering the work force. This has made the second peak of the M-curve higher.

ᐧ Furthermore, in the 1980s, women's average length of service in their companies climbed steadily as more women postponed quitting their jobs. Age at marriage and at first birth are being pushed back, and the number of births per woman is at an all-time low of 1.53 (Rōdōshō Fujin Kyoku 1992:42). These factors combine to make the M's trough increasingly shallow. Also, the span of years in between early retirement at marriage and reentry after child-rearing is decreasing. The notion that a woman's primary responsibility is to her home remains strong, however, and employment policies and practices, although gradually changing, are largely premised upon a male career mode. Examples of such practices are frequent job location transfer, expectations of after-hours socializing, heavy overtime schedules, long working hours in comparison with Europe and the United States, paucity of vacation time, and so on. These practices necessitate a great deal of commitment to one's job and are accompanied by the assumption that a man's spouse will take care of his household affairs entirely. The concept of full-time, career-oriented employee carries with it the expectation that this employee will be, first and foremost, a company man. Needless to say, it is a rare married woman employee who can rise to this standard and still have a family left to go home to. Thus we have the paradox that, although Japanese women have had certain rights guaranteed in the post–World War II Labor Standards Law to help them maintain continuous employment, a combination of cultural norms regarding male and female roles, and the nature of the expectations for career employees, has kept them from coming anywhere near the male pattern of job tenure. The aforementioned rights are pregnancy leave for twelve weeks, extended in 1989 to fourteen weeks, at 60 percent of one's pay, and child-care time, which allows a woman one-half an hour of rest twice a day during working hours to care for her infant, until the baby is two years old. Hence the trough in the M-curve, although filling in, still forms an M (see Figure 2).

We should also note that the older a woman is, the less likely she is to be employed by a large firm. Large firms, with higher wages and more benefits, generally do not encourage women to make careers of their jobs. The smaller the firm, the less selective it can afford to be regarding the age of its workers (see Figure 3).

In terms of the M-curve, most of my coworkers at Azumi were either in the trough of the M or at the second peak, trying not to slip down the slope until they reached retirement age. By virtue of being regular employees despite their status as housewives and mothers,

Figure 2. Women's Labor Power by Age, 1975–1985

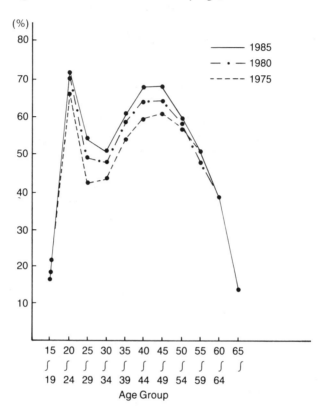

*Source:* From Sōmuchōtōkei Kyoku [Rōdōryoku Chōsa]; reprinted in Takenaka (1989), 289.

they were bucking the system. Married Azumi women who were staying on the line from age fifteen, as well as those who were mid-career entrants, had chosen a controversial career trajectory. Why?

Most took a job for economic reasons, whether to help pay for a house or condominium, or for educational or other child-related expenses. If the woman was divorced or widowed, however, she worked for the basic necessities; in households where there is no father present, the income of the mother alone is usually insufficient to provide for "extras" such as new appliances, a car, a house, or additional

Figure 3. Women Employees by Age and Size of Firm

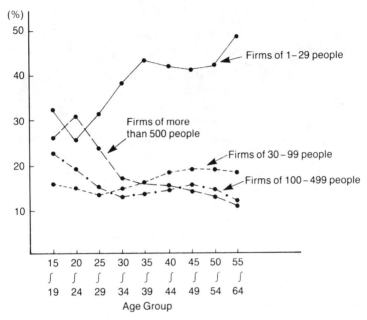

Source: From Sōmuchōtōkei Kyoku [Rōdōryoku Chōsa]; reprinted in Takenaka (1989), 294.

Note: The firms are nonagricultural, but no distinction has been made between public and private.

schooling for the children. My coworkers agreed that married women work to maintain a certain living standard. Even though they strive to keep up that level, however, some feel it is too high, and that people have given in to greed and extravagance. But all felt that their husband's salaries have not kept pace with the increase in the cost of living or with the higher standard of consumption. Shimizu san, a thirty-two-year-old mother of two who had been working at Azumi since graduating from junior high school, had this to say:

> . . . even if it's only a little, it helps out with the household finances. The standard of living has risen greatly. A house [that] didn't have a refrigerator ten years ago. . . . Now there's one in

every house, and a car for every two people, one per household. It's because we have these things and the living standard has risen that more and more people are working. . . .

Nishitani san, a married woman with two children and one on the way, focuses on the consequences of rising educational standards:

> . . . It's funny to call it luxury, but one wants spending money. People want videos and things. And we've come to spend money on kids that we didn't used to spend. Luxuries like home tutors, cram schools. Before it used to be OK just to send your child to the regular school program, but that's not good enough anymore. So if you want to give your child the same as the next, it costs money. Because luxury has become commonplace in our lives, we can't get by on just our husband's salaries, so we have to work. That's how my family is. We could get by on Father's (my husband's) salary alone, but we want more than that. We want to do this and that for the kids. Give them nice clothes and toys. At this point nice toys are enough, but once they get to elementary school, we want to give them supplemental education, and that takes money.

Nishitani san plans to quit the company as soon as her eldest child enters elementary school because she does not have access to after-school day care. But she says that then she will look for a job as a *paato*.

Kamida *hanchō* (group supervisor), a married thirty-seven-year-old mother of two who has been with Azumi since junior high, emphasizes the practical: it is a waste of resources to have a woman at home when she could be out working, especially in view of the cramped quarters typical of modern housing. Moreover, the *naishoku* market has shrunk, so if a woman wants to earn income, she almost has to go out:

> Well, household finances are probably a part of it, but it's a waste for women to just sit at home. For instance, nowadays when you talk about houses, it's a *danchi* [apartment complex]. There's hardly any women's work like washing and cleaning left to do. In the old days, it took a day to do the garden. Even *naishoku* isn't as available as it used to be. There aren't many kinds of *naishoku*. Since there are lots of people with spare time, they decide to work, even if only a little.

Kamida *hanchō* does not seem to be of the opinion held by most housewives in Imamura's (1987) study: that a housewife's main job is the education and care of her children. The point she emphasizes is the lack of productive work a housewife can accomplish when living in an apartment complex. To Kamida *hanchō,* this is a waste of her talents.

Others, while putting economic reasons first, also consider personal satisfaction a factor in women's decision to work. Fujii san comments:

> Well, prices have risen, but also, women have found the joy of working. Rather than being at home and aimlessly passing the time, if you put the kids in day care and go to work, you get the feeling that you are really alive. You're not just counting the years going by—five years, ten years—even if you have just one goal . . . if you're working you can have it be to save money to buy a house, for instance.

Few of my coworkers longed to be professional housewives. Of course, none of them were that when I talked to them. Those who longed for it were older and had been full-time housewives previously.

Many of the women had ambivalent feelings about the profession of housewife. They felt that it could constitute a complete and valuable job. For various reasons, however, they felt that they themselves were not suited to housewifery. One group supervisor, Usui san, a married woman with two children who was thirty-one with sixteen years of service (hired out of junior high school at age fifteen), made the following observations:

> U: I'd say it depends on how one thinks. There are those who like to work and those who stay in the household—if they think this is their job and they're satisfied with it, that's fine.
> G: Would you be satisfied with it?
> U: I'm not so sure. I'm the type who finds it hard to breathe staying in the same place all the time, so it's best for me to get out. I get depressed at home. I'm not suited to it.

Forty years old and unmarried, Murakami *kakarichō* (subsection chief) emphasized how being a housewife limits a woman's horizons:

> They must have resourceful men, right? The men must have good incomes. But as one woman looking at another, I think they are pitiable. When your only relationships are with the next-door

neighbor ladies, you don't know what's going on in the world, and your viewpoint doesn't expand. Conversation among wives is only about small things occurring in the immediate vicinity, right? So I pity them.

Another coworker noted that, since housewives have to operate within their husbands' salaries, there are those with extra and those with nothing to spare, and she pitied the latter. This point about the income a housewife must operate within is important. Although I have no hard data, my impression is that most of my coworkers would have had difficulty managing the budget on their husbands' income alone. If they stayed at home, they would not be emulating the upper-middle-class housewives of TV dramas who wear designer clothing, hire private tutors for their children, drive luxury-model cars, attend culture classes, meet at upscale cafés for lunch, and the like. Instead, they would be stuck in the house, in perhaps morally uplifting but depressing penury.

According to Nishitani san, a regular employee with sixteen years' service who, at thirty-two, had two children with a third on the way: "I envy them [she laughs]. But for me, I'm more suited to being outside. Three meals plus a nap sounds appealing, but I couldn't stand just doing housework. I want to have my own interests, and there are many things I want to study. I think it would be a lonely existence."

People often say that housewives have an easy life because their husbands support them—the job comes with three meals and a nap *(san shoku hirune tsuki)*. Perhaps this slightly derogatory image of professional housewives indicates a decline in the social assessment of their value. One rarely hears of *ryōsai kenbo* (good wife, wise mother) these days, but *san shoku hirune tsuki* is on the tip of many tongues, male and female.

What do the young unmarried think of the professional housewife? Of the few unmarried women I interviewed only one said she might like to become one. Irahara san, a twenty-four-year-old with nine years of service to the company, echoes the envy/pity reactions of others. She also has an unrealistic view of household life, not recognizing the hard work it entails:

> I: It's worthless!
> G: Why?
> I: Actually, I'm envious. No work, but they can eat and sleep, right? That must be the easiest life, huh? That's not for me. But I

do envy them. Everything all set for them. When their husband comes home, they just ask him, "Would you like your bath, or dinner?" That's the best. Isn't that the ideal home? But I wouldn't like it.

G: You mean it doesn't suit your personality?

I: It's better for me to be outside. I feel it'd be too gloomy to be in the house all the time. I like to talk with people a lot. Housewives only know household matters, and that's a pity. They should take more of a look at the world outside.

Another young woman, Murata san, accorded value to housewifery but thought that staying at home is a sure way to age rapidly:

They're trying their best to keep the home, so that's wonderful. People who work have to reconcile work and home, and that's very hard, but that's OK for them. I don't want to be a professional housewife. I'd like to work. You age quickly if you stay at home. You look like an old lady, an aunty.

This is an opinion often voiced—by going out to work, women stay youthful and pretty. Doi *kachō,* section chief at the Shipping Center Inspection and Packaging division, said the same thing when he told me that it is a good thing for housewives to work. They start paying attention to their hair, dress, and makeup, and they become more vivacious. In contrast, there is a darkness associated with women who stay at home. Women often told me that it would be gloomy to be at home all day, and they use verbs such as *tojikomoru* (to be shut in). They say that women who are housewives do not take care of themselves and look old before their time. Going out of the neighborhood requires dressing up, putting on one's outside face. My coworkers enjoyed this chance to put on a public demeanor, but they also noted its impact on the household budget. Yet now that more and more housewives are taking extradomestic employment, those who stay home are seen as dowdy.[1]

Last of all, some women say it is good to be a housewife while raising the children, but after they are grown one need not remain inside the house. Whether this is out of their personal conviction that it is best for the family if the wife quits her job and remains at home while the children are small, or whether most women recognize it would be extremely difficult to remain on the job throughout marriage and pregnancy, is open to question. My impression is that company atmosphere and job conditions, combined with deep-seated notions of women's role as primary caretakers of the family, impel the majority of Japanese women to quit at marriage or, increasingly, the birth of the first child. By now, however, it is common practice for women to reenter the work force later.

As we have seen, most of my coworkers did not wish to follow the professional housewife model themselves, and some even ridiculed it. They were a far cry from the elite women studied by Iwao Sumiko (1993:268) who "still conspire to use men as the worker bees of society." Whether or not they subscribed to that vision of women's role, however, their lives were affected by it in many ways. Their full-time status challenged the professional housewife ideal, an ideal upon which the company had based its hiring, promotion, and retirement practices for women. What were these practices, how did notions of gender inform them, and what effects did they have on women's careers?

## Recruitment

On the company side, the selection process for female factory employees was simple, consisting of tests of dexterity and basic arithmetic, followed by an interview. As is typical for both sexes in Japan, these women were trained on the job after entering the company; few had special training of any kind before taking the job. Some had learned sewing in school, however, or in previous jobs. After entering the company, they learned by watching and copying experienced people. Usually new employees were assigned to a more experienced person to teach them the job.

When I asked the submanager of the personnel department what sort of young woman Azumi sought for factory employment, he said they took girls from mediocre schools who did not like school and were not high achievers. This type of girl would presumably be more suited to the tedium of the factory. They all entered as F (*futsū*, ordinary) group workers, and the management did not expect or desire them to go beyond that group, as they did male workers. He candidly remarked, "Once you learn the job, that's it—you won't become *buchō* or *shachō*."

From the F group they might move to the G group (*gijutsu*, skilled) if they gained skill in sewing. Office women were also in the G group.

The pay scales for these two groups were similar and increased by step: F1, F2, G1, G2, and so on. Few factory women made the transition to the K group (*kikaku kaihatsu,* planning and development), which was required for any supervisory position above *hanchō* (group leader). To do this one had to be recommended to take an exam. The head of the Inspection and Packaging Division, Murakami *kakarichō,* is one who made this transition.

In the sixties, newly employed junior-high-school graduates were trained in large groups before actually starting their jobs. Shimizu san, who entered the company in 1967, explains:

> When I entered the company, it was with a group of fifty women who all received the same instruction together. That training included Azumi's company history, sewing machine use, and so on. It lasted two months. I entered at the age of fourteen, when I graduated from junior high, and have continued to the present. I entered in 1967, so it's been seventeen years. I came from a poor family and couldn't afford to continue with my education, so when my teacher suggested Azumi, I agreed. I lived in Fushimi and was very naive about the world, so I really had no basis on which to choose a job. I took a test with one other girl, and only then did I realize exactly what sort of company it was. My father was a tailor and I was interested in sewing myself, so I was glad it was clean work. But it was only after I entered that I realized that Azumi was a company that made women's lingerie!

According to Shimizu san, 1965–1967 were the years when the most junior-high graduates entered the company, and groups of fifty to one hundred girls entered simultaneously. At that time, the type of work was determined by educational level, with junior-high graduates learning manual work while high-school graduates were sent to do office work. Those who entered from junior high were given the opportunity to attend night school to obtain their high-school equivalency diplomas; three of the women I knew had participated in this program. One described it as a very enjoyable and worthwhile experience, so much so that she wanted to continue on to college. Another, who did not make it through, commented that it was extremely tiring to work days and attend night school, and she could not keep up.

As Shimizu san indicates, the company recruited through the local junior high schools at this time, and those who entered directly after graduation from junior or senior high school often found out about Azumi through recruitment books at the school, or teachers who had connections with the company recommended Azumi to the student. This connection between teacher and student is sometimes sustained even after the initial introduction to the company, as we can see from one young woman's experience.[2] Kamida san entered Azumi in 1962 on the advice of her junior-high-school teacher. During her first year on the job she was disgusted with the malicious teasing she encountered and wanted to quit, but was counseled to stick it out: "I couldn't stand it and went to my teacher to complain, but the teacher told me that it'd be the same no matter where I went, so finally I stood it for one year, and now it's been twenty!"

Most of my coworkers, whether fresh out of school or mid-career entrants, chose Azumi more for the glamour of its image, its solid reputation, and the size of the company than from any detailed knowledge of the actual work, salary, or benefits. Company size, in particular, was important, since it meant there was little likelihood that the company would go bankrupt in the foreseeable future, and bonuses would be higher than at small or medium-sized firms.

## Changes in Recruitment

As Japan recovered from the postwar devastation, the company began to have difficulty in recruiting at the level of the junior-high graduate, due to the shift upward in education. At this point it began to recruit high-school graduates for factory jobs; moreover, it began to hire middle-aged women as both regular employees and *paato*. Hasegawa san, a married woman who was hired at age forty-two, explained: "In 1974, Azumi didn't care whether you were young or old. Everywhere in Japan was having a labor shortage. Not like now." These middle-aged entrants usually found out about the job through newspaper ads or through friends or acquaintances who worked at the company. Like new school graduates, they had to take a manual dexterity and arithmetic test and were interviewed before being hired.

Even with a labor shortage, however, the company did have an age limit of forty-two on hiring. This is a legal and common practice in Japanese firms, but it appears that this age limit was fairly negotiable. Nakanishi san explains how she managed to get a job in the company at age forty-four:

I started at Azumi in 1976, in November. I never dreamed at that age that they'd let me in as a regular employee, but I really wanted to work at Azumi and I had a friend—not a good friend, but a friend—introduce me. The *kachō* said I was too old at forty-four and should give up; it was a 98 percent chance that I wouldn't get in. So I gave up. But the *kachō* told her to bring in my resume anyway, even though it'd probably be of no use. Then he asked me to come in and try. How happy I was! I never dreamed of it—I was forty-four, and they said they were only taking up to forty-two.

Besides having an established connection who worked at Azumi, contributing factors in Nakanishi san's case could have been the proximity of her home to the company—a mere five-minute walk—and her previous ten years' experience as a *naishoku* (working inside the home) seamstress.

In the sixties and early seventies, a person entering as a *paato* often had the opportunity of becoming a regular employee after a trial period. Kushida san, one of the *paato* with whom I worked in the Inspection and Packaging Section, comments on this, and on the reasons she preferred not to become a regular employee:

I heard about Azumi hiring temporary help—a friend working at Azumi introduced me. It was only a one-month contract. I took the job because it was temporary. My child was sick, so I couldn't accept a job as a regular employee. But it lasted ten years. The people who entered with me all became *shain* (regular employees) —first, for six months or a year, they'd be *paato* and then they became *shain*. It depended on the person; those who continued without taking any holidays were made *shain*. But my child was in the hospital. The child commuted to school from the hospital and wasn't at home. I had to go for meetings twice a month. So I had to take time off. If you're a *shain* you have to be awfully careful about taking time off. Since I knew ahead of time that I had to take time off, I couldn't very well become a *shain* then.

Kushida san continued as a *paato* at Azumi for over ten years, until (her contract was not renewed) she was dismissed when the I&P moved from the factory to the shipping center.

The company also hired handicapped people as regular employees, starting in the 1970s, as required by law for a company over a certain size. Taniguchi san, a forty-eight-year-old worker in the I&P Division, was hired in 1976 during a drive to recruit handicapped people as regular employees. She had had infantile paralysis, which left her with poor motor coordination, but she was able to walk without mechanical aids. Before getting the job at Azumi, her previous job experience had been at a small necktie shop, which fired her during a business slump. She had also worked for her family's business, making Christmas ornaments, but they went bankrupt after the oil shock in 1974. Taniguchi san explained what happened then:

> The work I had before entering Azumi was at a company that makes neckties. And because of the bad economic times . . . how should I explain . . . because it went into a decline they had to reduce the staff. Just at that time I saw in the newspaper that they needed applications from handicapped people. I had thought it would be great if I could enter a big company like that. Azumi was becoming very famous worldwide. But they had not included the handicapped in their hiring. It just happened that there was a recruiting call for handicapped people. So I applied.

## Gender Stratification

Promotion is available to both sexes, but for women the concentration is at lower levels where women supervise other women. In 1984 there was one woman subsection chief in the factory. Two subsection chiefs, all three section chiefs, and the factory manager were men. As noted previously, less than 10 percent of the factory employees (18 out of 242) were men.

For the corporation as a whole, 3 percent of all female employees, 97 women, held positions of rank. Of these, six were section heads or higher; 91 were in positions such as *shisutaa, insutorakutaa,* and *hanchō.* Most of the male employees, (880, or 68 percent) held positions of rank, and 123 (14 percent) of these were section head or higher. This was in a corporation where women made up roughly two-thirds of the work force. This is not unusual. The National Institute of Employment and Vocational Research (1988:45) noted:

> In the case of men, career development proceeds under an assumption of long service, and promotion is made to higher positions with service years, while such a system is not generally established for women. In other words, male workers are considered a part of the

seniority-oriented promotion system, while female workers are put outside this framework, and only the few blessed with the opportunity and abilities are singled out.

The institute adds that although more and more companies are promoting women, only 56.3 percent of companies surveyed said they offered promotional opportunities of any kind to women. Azumi is one that does promote women, and most recently (1989–1990) has been opening up more opportunities for women workers than existed in the early 1980s. This is mainly attributable to two factors. First, the Equal Employment Opportunity Act, which came into effect in 1986, stipulates that companies have an obligation to make efforts to provide women with equal opportunities in both training and promotion. Second, as we shall see in Chapter 2, more and more women at Azumi are staying on in their jobs, not leaving at marriage or childbirth. The management sees the need to give these veteran workers opportunities for advanced training and responsibility if the company is to do well in the coming years.

Even now, few if any Azumi women would become *buchō* or *shachō,* but not for lack of talent. In fact, I met some very capable and intelligent women at the factory. Some had been recognized by management for their abilities and had gone as far as women were generally allowed to go—to *hanchō* (supervisor) or instructor of sewing. Others, despite their abilities, had never been promoted beyond *shisutaa.* Ota san (age forty, twenty-five years' service, married with two children) remarked:

> O: There is a big difference between men and women as regards their responsibility and their pay. Partly it's the women's own fault. But I think these things need improvement.
>
> G: Could you be more specific?
>
> O: For instance, I've worked for twenty-three years, and . . . properly speaking, I should be a *kakarichō* by now, not just be in a different job [than when I started out]. I'm nowhere near [being a *kakarichō*]—I'm the same regular status I always was.

Ota san is not only dissatisfied with her own status, but sees this as a general problem of the company's failure to assign women positions involving business management:

> O: For instance, management *(eigyō)* type work is made out to be men's work. As long as they have the ability, women can do

any work, but the company doesn't give women those kinds of work or those workplaces.

G: You mean supervisory work?

O: I mean running the business. There are many kinds of work which are thought to be for men and not given to women. It's not a case of her being able to do it if she has ability; it's a case of her having ability plus not losing out to the man—then she could do it.

Other women also said that they would like to try their hand at many different kinds of work, like the men, but the company would not allow it. When I asked if she thought there was any difference between men and women in working conditions, Fujii san (age twenty-eight, thirteen years' service, two children) replied:

Yes . . . it's difficult. Sometimes there is a test you can take if you want. It'd be great if you could get them to treat you the same as a man if you passed it, but actually you can't really get them to recognize you in the same way. I have trouble with that sort of thing. Because your credentials anyway are the same, men and women. Since we both entered the workplace having passed the same exam, I want them to consider me on the same basis as the men.

Ota san apportions blame to both the company and the women workers themselves. When I asked her, "If there are any problems at your workplace, what are they?" she replied:

This company is big, and with so many women workers, they should make it easier for women to work here. The women themselves, too, should ask more of their jobs. They shouldn't just be content with what they're given to do. They should have more and more expectations about their work. Otherwise nothing will ever come of it. Although there are many women in the factory, the ones who direct them are a tiny group of men—they're moving the whole works. I think that it won't become an easier place for women to work unless women also participate in management.

When she assigned part of the blame to women, Ota san referred to the myriad problems confronting the ambitious—jealousy, rivalry, the feeling that one should not be too outspoken, the feeling that one should not be too different from the rest. One of the shipping-center managers said that he sends women with ability to the main office because their enthusiasm gets quashed by their coworkers at the shipping center. He told me that women who excel, who are too interested in their work, are thought of as odd ducks. Other women discourage them from being too ambitious.

One of three nurses I interviewed commented on the company's failure to develop the talents of the women workers:

> I think there still is a lot of discrimination against women who work in this society. We're still far away from equality of opportunity. Women's ability is underestimated on account of their being women. The social structure itself is that of a society where men work. It's not becoming a place where conditions are favorable for women to work. If women think of working, first they run up against the wall of marriage and household. Then it's child-rearing. There's a big difference there (between men and women). . . . I suppose since she's the mother, it's something a woman must do, but . . . there's the big clincher. I don't think there's any discrimination in education, and even physically, except for really heavy labor, there's no difference between men and women— women aren't weak. I'd like women to be given equal opportunity. The problem is, after you enter the company, treatment is different for women and men. The company, thinking the man will be there his whole life, scrambles to give him training and opportunities. But these are not given to women. They can't get trained and are marginalized from the start.

The company expected men to treat their jobs as lifetime careers, and to retire at the age of fifty-five. (In 1985 the age was raised to sixty.) For younger women, the company expected and preferred them to quit upon marriage, or at least upon the birth of the first child. The company saw young married women, especially those with children, as reducing productivity, and complained that they lose interest in work, lack ambition, and are frequently late or absent. It attributed these negative traits to their inability to reconcile their roles as wives and mothers with their roles as workers.

The desire to have women quit upon marriage is not solely linked to material considerations, however. As we saw in the philosophy of Azumi's president, it is directly related to cultural values concerning motherhood and what form the role of mother should take. The managers with whom I discussed this topic echoed the company president's concern that the society would crumble if more and more mothers continued to work, especially when their children were of preschool age. They feared that the children would not be well cared for, auguring ill for Japan's future.[3] Such attitudes, combined with a demanding work structure with little flexibility, meant that Azumi's working women faced many difficulties.

Azumi has hired several women (like Kushida san; see Chap. 1) who have reentered the labor force after their children have grown. Management does not consider these to be career jobs, nor does it expect the women to continue until retirement. In fact, it prefers them to quit by about age fifty, since after that most women have trouble keeping pace in the jobs to which they are assigned, most of which involve fine work demanding excellent eyesight, coordination, and concentration.

## Women's Aspirations toward Promotion

Perhaps the knowledge that their chances for rising very high in the ranks of the company were slim and experience of the difficulties of combining a challenging job with household responsibilities led to women's lack of aspiration toward promotion. Although I asked women if they considered opportunities for promotion in their evaluation of a job's worth, almost everyone answered that she did not think of such things. Fujii san, whom we earlier heard express a desire to be considered on a par with men, said: "I don't think of such things. Maybe it's funny for me to say that as long as I can work it's OK, but I don't have any desire to climb."

I might add here that one could not take a test for promotion without the recommendation of one's superior. Whereas some superiors are glad to recognize a woman's potential and invite her to take the test, most are not.[4] Moreover, I heard reports of discrimination, particularly against individuals who had engaged in any objectionable political activities, such as affiliation with the Japan Communist party. In such cases promotion would be delayed, if it came at all. This was more of a problem in the 1960s, for most of the Communists at Azumi have been weeded out by now.

Tahara san told me that in the early days, when there were many employees and the company was booming, promotion for employees (even women up to a certain level) was more or less automatic and tests were easy. In her words:

> Now it's extremely difficult, but at that time, because they were short of hands, you perfunctorily went up the ladder . . . if you were the kind who went against some company policy, or that sort of thing, and wrote or said something about it, you would be passed over, but if this were not the case, then it was fairly smooth. At that time, and still to some extent, there were these Communist types who went against the company. You know, the kind who say things like, "Since you're making such a profit, how about giving us a raise?" and that sort of thing. There are people who whisper such things in the shadows. How can I explain it? There's the Communist *Minsei*, the Democratic Youth organization. It's in the Communist party. And there are people [in Azumi] who belong to that group. They do it secretly as a group. And it appears that the company investigates such people. It takes longer for those sorts of people to get to take the test. Naturally, the company looks into those things.

It seems reasonable to conclude that Ota san, the veteran of twenty-five years who complained that she ought to be a *kakarichō* by now, is one of those who never went far in the company because of her political beliefs and her activities in trying to inform and organize workers to improve working conditions. Despite her obvious intelligence and dedication to her job, it took her ten years to become a *shisutaa*, and she was never promoted again.

I began this chapter with a presentation by Azumi's president extolling the virtues of the professional housewife and warning of the dangers of any other gender role for Japanese women. Azumi was built on the premise that eager young women would enter the company, work for several years, perhaps gaining the rank of *shisutaa*, or even *insutorakutaa* or *hanchō*, then marry and retire to their true professions as wives and mothers. They did not want high flyers; such women could not well be accommodated in a promotion system with such a low ceiling. Those two I knew to make the grade to *kakarichō*, Murakami san and Tahara san, were anomalies: the former remained single; the latter, divorced.

The system was orderly as far as it went, but when young women at the first peak of the M began pushing the limits, there was no place for them in this order. Furthermore, when the company, desperate for workers, hired middle-aged married women as regular employees, this added stress to a system already in trouble. It both challenged the very cultural assumptions upon which Azumi had based its personnel practices and upset power relations in a hierarchically oriented culture. One might think it absurd that the president of the same company which hired these women was lecturing to them that married women belong in the home, but the gender role model that had worked fine in an earlier era was definitely out of sync with the economy of the 1980s, and the managers had not foreseen, nor did most of them approve of, the changes that were taking place. Contradictions abounded. My coworkers themselves were not necessarily without doubts about the choices they were making to be married employees. Work on the shop floor was all the more challenging for such women, because it contradicted a gender role model to which they themselves subscribed, at least to some extent. And, often those who did feel justified in stretching women's gender model to include work after marriage did not feel that it was desirable for women to strive for promotion beyond the lower levels. As I mentioned earlier, women sometimes even held other women back from achieving (see also Chaps. 5 and 6). Few blue-collar women were as critical of the company's practices regarding promotion as was Ota san, who probably had had a dose of ideological orientation from the Communist party. The nurses I interviewed also had a more critical eye, but their positions offered them a wider view of the overall situation, and they had much more education than most of my coworkers.

Chapter 2 will examine the challenges of work on the shop floor, and strategies my coworkers used to meet them. We shall also see how those who could not "take it" had little choice but to quit.

# 2

# *The Daily Challenge: Cope or Quit?*

To an outsider, work at the Inspection and Packaging Section would seem tedious at best. Inspection and packaging both involve repetition of quick movements, with little variation. The "downside" of lifetime employment, especially when most of one's career is spent working on a limited number of tasks, became readily apparent to me. Our lives were circumscribed by a number of rules, many unwritten: run, don't walk to the restroom; work through your break if you're falling behind; be ready to begin work before the bell rings. It took me some time to learn how to behave in an acceptable manner, to learn which rules were negotiable and which were not. Ultimately, repeated unacceptable behavior led employees to have to quit.

At Azumi, women were constantly challenged to maintain a very high standard of quality. In a sense, their status as regular employees was earned daily by meeting production targets and quality standards. This required a disciplined work force. This chapter will discuss the ways in which discipline was maintained at the I&P: how we were encouraged to fall in line and what happened when we fell out of line.

Let me give an example. Personalizing one's space was not allowed; Murakami *kakarichō* wished to emphasize our alikeness. Unlike in the "Stitchco" workshop that Westwood (1984) studied in England, Azumi's workers did not decorate their work areas with pictures of home and children, photos of animals, or cutouts from magazines. The *kakarichō* considered any cluttering of the work area with personal items of any sort as being disorderly and unbusinesslike. We were enjoined to keep home and work separate. The only decorations on the walls were pictures of fashion models wearing Azumi products. Whereas in Westwood's workplace women made colorful aprons out of fabric scraps from work and wore them over their regular clothing, at the I&P everyone had to wear the same company uniform, and no one was to adorn it.

I learned this the hard way when, one winter day, I put on a sweater over my uniform to ward off the chill from the blast of wind coming through the wide-open delivery door. The *shisutaa* in charge rushed over when she saw me, telling me to take it off, as it was *kakkō warui* (it didn't look good). I told her I had it on because I was cold, but if it was not permitted, I would take it off. She went back to consult the *kakarichō* and returned to say if I wanted to wear the sweater I would have to put it on *under* my uniform. Moreover, in order to execute this maneuver, I should go to the back of the room where no one was, and stoop down beneath the table to hide from view. By this time I felt the whole matter was pretty ridiculous and opted for goose bumps.

Taniguchi san later came to tell me that she had overheard the whole thing and to reassure me of her support. She said if anyone was *kakkō warui* it was the *shisutaa* herself, who was wearing a red plaid blanket over her hips to keep warm during her period. I, too, had seen the irony in this, but hesitated to point it out to the *shisutaa*. Perhaps warding off culturally meaningful chills, such as those which come with menstruation, is acceptable, whereas insisting on wearing a sweater just because of a brief blast of cold air is not.

When individuality was asserted against company rules, it was often covert. For instance, one cold morning Hasegawa san, an I&P inspector, brought in a miniature bottle of whiskey to lace her morning coffee. During the prework morning breakfast gathering she offered it to us surreptitiously, cautioning us not to let any of the supervisors see, as drinking during work was forbidden.

In another case, one day my group was set to the task of making boxes with tissue-paper inserts. The supervisor instructed us to divide the task among us, some of us folding boxes, others inserting tissue, and so on. There was a large quantity to be done, and we realized that those put to folding boxes were rapidly getting sore hands, so we decided to trade off folding and inserting. When the supervisor came to check up on us, she insisted that her method was more efficient, so we complied—until she went back to her desk. Then, without saying a word, my coworkers reverted to doing the job their way. There was no confrontation; they did not try to convince the supervisor that their method was better. They simply obeyed her when she was present and did it their way when she was not. Direct challenges to authority were much less frequent. (We shall find them in Chapter 4.)

Taniguchi san, who had difficulties in movement and speech as a result of a childhood disease, had to work at a slow and steady pace, and she welcomed any chance that came her way to take it a little bit easy. She was quite clear about this one day when we were stamping the cardboard inserts for the plastic bags for bodysuits. This was one job that could be done sitting down, and was quite pleasant as jobs go, requiring little expenditure of effort. It also called for little concentration, so we were able to chat while working. As we neared the end of the lot, Taniguchi san cautioned me not to go so fast, or we would run out of work and they'd give us something harder to do! I was shocked to hear such a comment from an Azumi employee, although at an American factory where I had once worked such sentiments were often voiced. Although her pace was slow, however, Taniguchi san's work was never slipshod, and if she made a mistake, she was always terribly remorseful. She wanted to do a good job, and if she resorted to such tactics in order to get a rest, it did not reflect a poor attitude toward her work, but rather her determination to keep up with a normal pace that was beyond her physical limitations.

There were also other employees who seemed to lack the zest that characterized the work style of most women I observed. Two of them, I learned later, had chronic illnesses and were undergoing medical treatment; one was moonlighting as a bar hostess (an infraction of employment regulations) and was suffering from lack of sleep. It was commonly accepted that one owed the company a solid day of work. There was an unofficial minimum standard of production, and those who failed to meet it were resented not only by the company management but also by their fellow workers, in part because they would have to take up the slack. The minimum standard was unofficial in the sense that the targets were assigned according to an individual's ability and gradually adjusted upward. They were not linked to basic monthly pay, and those who fell behind the target were not penalized. Differences in individual performance were taken into account at bonus time and in promotion decisions. Moreover, especially at the factory, it was made obvious who was excelling and who was falling behind: every day we were required to chart how many pieces we had completed in how much time; this record was posted for all to see. Each morning the *kakarichō* would announce the names of those who had met their targets from the previous day and would honor them with a "Gokurōsan deshita!" ("Thank you for your effort").

Along with everyone else at the factory's I&P, I was given my individual target, which I found impossible to meet consistently. I could achieve it only at my top speed, which I could not maintain even for the half-day that I worked. My coworkers left me behind in the dust. I finally managed by working at a slow but regular pace, unless it was a really busy day, and concentrated on accuracy rather than speed, which was hopelessly out of my reach. This work style would not have been acceptable had I been a Japanese employee, and it did not fail to attract the attention of my colleagues, one of whom, after our interview, asked me if all Americans work at "my pace" (meaning a self-determined pace) like I do!

## Aiming for Perfection

The goods produced by Azumi's home factory had the lowest rate of return of unsatisfactory products of all Azumi's factories. The women in the I&P were proud of this record, for in some measure it was due to their diligence: they were responsible for the final inspection before each item went to the shops. However, like any record, it was harder to maintain than to achieve. At I&P, the *kakarichō* had devised certain methods to prompt those who were furthest from perfection to become closer to it. Among these were the *hansei* (a public apology for one's mistakes, which included a self-reflection on why one had committed the error and what one planned to do to prevent it from happening again)[1] and public apologies for all absences. Everyone thought the practices too harsh, but the only solutions were individual: to challenge oneself to try even harder, to rationalize that no job is easy, to realize that every place has its good and bad points and one must put up with the bad ones, and/or to handle frustrations by talking them over with work companions. The last resort, of course, was to quit.

Let us consider each of these coping methods in turn. Ogawa san told me that a problem generally faced by workers in the I&P section, particularly by the inspectors, was how to deal with errors in quality control. In her words:

We are in the Inspection and Packaging Section, and that is the most important work. If you overlook one flaw in any of the lots they check, they send them all back to us. Then they look at the chit and see whose work it was. Then you really get it. Inspection, like anything else, *looks* easy, but actually it's the most tiring. Even if you make an error, you must keep doing inspection. Because of that, some people in I&P think . . . [that it's unfair that inspectors have it so rough, as compared with packagers]. If you make one more mistake they'll get that much more mad at you. Now it's not so bad (with the change in *kakarichō*)—it depends on who the boss is, too. But it was awful. Many people quit because of that. They totally lost confidence.

I asked her if it was the new people who had quit. She replied:

Even old hands like me—even we have times when we don't feel so great. Say they happen to find something you inspected when you weren't feeling well. Then they know who did it immediately. It comes back, and you have to read your self-criticism at the morning ceremony, in front of everyone. You tell the *shisutaa* your self-criticism and say: "Because I did it X way I overlooked the defect. From now on I won't do it X way. I'll do it Y way." Well, you can get away with it once or twice. But if you keep making mistakes, you run out of things to say. After two or three times, it doesn't wash anymore. And that is very harsh.

I asked her if this policy had been in effect for a long time. She answered:

No. It's because everyone kept making mistakes. So three and a half years ago Murakami *kakarichō* decided [to implement it]. It's only in the I&P . . . Sometimes you can't find the defects—threads that should have been cut off, and so on. Then they yell at you for it. And then your number of pieces finished starts to fall, and they call you down again. It's really unbearable. So it's a matter of how much you can win over yourself. Because they won't let you just go home. I went through a period like that. Everybody does. No matter how much you look, you overlook something. At that time, something happened that I'll never forget as long as I'm working here. At the morning ceremony, Murakami *kakarichō* said—not to me—not to wring your own neck (so to speak) over a single bra. When I heard that I was struck. I guess I felt, "Oh, I really must try hard." Because I *had* thought of quitting the company over just one bra. When she said not to do something that would amount to wringing one's own neck all on account of one bra, it gave me courage. I'm thinking of telling Murakami *kakari-chō* at the farewell party[2] that I can't forget those words. If I do tell her, she may start crying, I'll bet. Even now I can't forget. So when you're really down, one word from a superior can make you all right again, and make you feel like trying again. It's very important.

Two things struck me about this testimony. One is that although Ogawa san considered the lot of the inspectors a hard one, she did not put the blame totally on the policies of the *kakarichō*, who was urging speed plus quality control—rather strange bedfellows. Instead of blaming the supervisor for an unreasonable policy, she accepted the challenge and turned it into a personal battle to maintain self-confidence despite the occasional unavoidable error and the inevitable public *hansei*. Ogawa san even felt grateful to her supervisor for a word of encouragement and vowed to make greater efforts henceforth. Ogawa san also had a personal reason for resisting the urge to quit: her husband had not wanted her to work in the first place, and it would have been admitting defeat on two fronts if she had succumbed.

## Giving Up

Not all employees were as successful as Ogawa san in handling this challenge. As she reported, many women quit. Young women who quit because they found the work too demanding were able to find other jobs in smaller companies, presumably without too much difficulty (these were often in Azumi's network). I was able to interview two of the women who had formerly worked at Azumi and had been able to get jobs at one of the company's subsidiary firms nearby. They said the work was not nearly as difficult and the demands on their time were much less, but the pay was also much lower.

One of the women, Nakayama san, had quit at age twenty-four after working at Azumi for nine years. Two years prior to quitting she had been ordered to become a *shisutaa*. She did not really want to take on the responsibility, but felt she would probably learn something from the experience, so she agreed to it despite her unease. Once she became a *shisutaa,* she found that in order to get her work done she had to stay after work every day until 7:30 or 8:00 P.M. The extra hours were not counted as overtime. She could not stand the lack of personal time, so she quit. An employee of the subsidiary who frequented Azumi on business noticed her absence and contacted her, trying to persuade her to join the subsidiary. Nakayama san said that she had never supposed she would go back to doing the same work as before, but within three months of quitting, there she was. Her only dissatisfactions about the job were that the pay and benefits were markedly inferior to those of Azumi, and that work was less well organized. She saw this as inevitable in a small firm.

In Nakayama san we have the case of a young worker who quit of her own volition after deciding she wanted a less demanding job so that she could pursue personal interests. Others, though, quit when they receive the *katatataki,* the tap on the shoulder signaling that they have outworn their welcome. The closest I came to hearing the details of an incident that culminated in the employee's resignation was an unsolicited account of a case by Hasegawa san. Hasegawa san was comparing the shipping center to the factory when she first raised the topic:

> H: At the shipping center, even to men (who don't know much about how to do inspection) they say right then and there, "You do it like this," and then they just leave you alone and they make you do inspection just like that. That'd be unheard of at the factory. There, if you did that, people would make mistakes, and they'd return the defective goods. You'd have to do self-reflection. Then if you still made mistakes and defective products came back, it'd be the end. You'd have to quit eventually.
>
> G: Really? Things like that happen?
>
> K: Yes. Kinami san—do you know her? She was in Azumi before even Murakami was. Over thirty years. She always did inspection. She kept making mistakes.
>
> G: Was she sick?
>
> K: No, she wasn't sick. But she wasn't good at self-reflection— she was a poor talker. So she had to stand one whole day at the doors of the I&P Section. It became a big issue.
>
> G: Murakami *kakarichō* made her?
>
> K: It was when Sakurai san was *shisutaa.* Murakami san

ordered Sakurai to make her do it. She made her stand one day outside of the office until she could make a self-reflection. But it was too humiliating, because people come in and out. She stood the whole time but in the end she couldn't bear it. She ran away home. She did come back—her younger sister brought her and said, "Since it was her fault, she says she regrets it and will try hard, so please take her back." She even came with her younger sister! She started work again, but as you'd expect, she made mistakes. And when she did, they really put her through the wringer. That was the bad thing about the factory. Then you get so that you can't yield anymore. There's nothing you can do but quit. They treat you in such a way that you will eventually quit, because they can't *tell* you to quit. And so, in the end, she quit. There are lots of people who quit like that at the factory. At the I&P Section, there used to be three times as many people as there were when you came in. Almost all of them quit for such reasons. That's right. You're forced into quitting by what they do to you. If they tried treating me like that I'd stand up for myself. If they told *me* to stand all day and reflect, I'd go to the newspapers or the factory manager. For "reflection"—punishing people by making them stand—they can't do something like that. The factory manager was bad, too. He saw it but said nothing.

G: He knew about it?

K: Yes, he did. He saw but pretended not to. If that happened to me, I'd tell the newspapers. Then Azumi's name would be dragged through the mud.

G: A top-ranking company does things like that?

K: If they did such things to me, I'd quit then and there and go to the newspapers or someplace. But she was meek, not like an ordinary person. So she didn't do it. You didn't know about it? You never heard?

G: No.

Two other coworkers mentioned the incident to me on other occasions, using it to illustrate how strict the I&P had been. Although it had aroused the indignation of many, and although the women with whom I spoke about it said that they felt the treatment of this employee to have been unjustly severe, no one publicly censured the action at the time, and the union apparently did not come to the employee's aid.

Taniguchi san also brought up the case of Kinami san once in conversation, while we were at a coffee shop. Her version is similar but more detailed. According to her, when Kinami san began making a series of mistakes, she finally ran out of excuses for *hansei*. She got sick of writing them and stopped. Then the *shisutaa* told Murakami *kakarichō* that Kinami san had stopped writing *hansei*, so Murakami san directly ordered her to. For a few more days Kinami san still did nothing. In Taniguchi san's opinion, at this point she should have requested permission to take the vacation days she had coming to her —two full weeks. She was a serious worker who never missed a day unless she was ill. But Kinami san did not ask for a vacation, nor did Murakami *kakarichō* suggest that she take one. Also, Taniguchi san felt that the *shisutaa* or Murakami *kakarichō* should have given Kinami san different work to do for a while until she got over her problem; but they did not. So, on the third day of no *hansei*, Murakami *kakarichō* told Kinami san to stand outside the doors of the division until she felt she could write a *hansei*.[3] She stood there all day, through breaks, and did not even go to lunch until Murakami *kakarichō* told her to. The next day it was the same for half a day. Finally, Murakami *kakarichō* told Kinami san to go back to work, but first to apologize individually to each person in the section for having caused them extra work. She did it but quit soon after, telling Taniguchi san she could not stand coming to work any longer. She left before the summer bonus and without taking her vacation days.

Taniguchi san thought that both the *kakarichō* and Kinami san were at fault in this affair. Murakami *kakarichō* should have given Kinami san a vacation and/or a different sort of work temporarily; Kinami san should not have been so obstinate about the *hansei*. In any case, it was not a proper action to shame Kinami san by making her stand outside the doors like that, where visitors could see her.

Taniguchi san seemed to assign almost equal responsibility for the events to both parties, whereas Hasegawa san sided with the employee. Moreover, Hasegawa san said nothing about the various means by which Murakami *kakarichō* and Kinami san might have handled the situation and avoided the outcome, rather stressing the injustice of the circumstances. The focus of her outrage is that the company will stop at nothing to force a person to quit, even to the point of making the employee lose face. Although both would agree that Murakami *kakarichō*'s way of punishing Kinami san was reprehensible, Taniguchi san thinks that Kinami san should have forced herself to write something in order to avoid a crisis, whereas Hasegawa san acknowledges the absurdity of writing repeated *hansei*, sees Kinami san's insubordination as understandable, and proceeds to the next stage, which was her decision to follow Murakami *kakarichō*'s order. Here, she feels that Kinami san should have refused, quit on the spot, and taken revenge through the only avenue possible—the newspapers. However, Hasegawa san said that Kinami san was too weak to do this, and it is the weak who lose.

One might ask what made Kinami san lose the courage she must have had in order to refuse to write the *hansei* in the first place. Perhaps, after refusing, she realized how difficult the situation was and tried to show good faith by following Murakami *kakarichō*'s order to stand outside the doors. Or perhaps by following Murakami's orders she was indicating that she would do whatever work assigned her but was simply no longer capable of writing *hansei*. I can only speculate. What I can say with certainty is that the union did not become involved in the action—hardly surprising in view of the fact that the union shop representative was the very same *shisutaa* who had brought Kinami san's refusal to the attention of the *kakarichō* in the first place, a clear conflict of interest in American terms. Nor did Kinami san's fellow employees, who obviously felt sorry for her, come to her aid. Kinami san lost, for she ended up without job, bonus, or paid vacation. Most important, in Hasegawa san's opinion, she did not even achieve the satisfaction of revenge.

More than anything else, the above account illustrates the tenuous nature of even a regular employee's status once the company decides she is undesirable. Because the company is theoretically committed to the idea of lifetime employment and has entered into a relationship of mutual trust—*sōgo shinrai*—with the employee, it will not dismiss an employee unless s/he has committed some grave breach of contract. A decline in quality or slowing of work pace is not considered sufficient reason to dismiss an employee in Japan. Hanami (1979:89) notes: "The Courts have adopted a rather strict attitude towards admitting the existence of a 'just cause' [for dismissal of an employee]. From the general trend of the legal precedents it would seem that Japanese employers are not allowed to dismiss workers just because of their inefficiency, laziness or any minor misconduct."

Thus, a regular job is almost a kind of property possessed by the employee. Since it is difficult to dismiss a worker, employers find means to "have them quit" instead. The workers realized this, and the subject was often brought up in conversation. Especially for "immobile" workers,[4] it was an ever-present source of anxiety. Cole (1971:117–122) discusses the problem of dismissal and cites various ways that companies have of getting employees to quit without actually firing them outright. He refers to these tactics, such as frequent job transfers or the threat of them and assignment to low-status or dead-end jobs, as "functional equivalents" to firing. At the I&P, the humiliation of repeated *hansei* seems to have been an effective equivalent to firing.

I have mentioned the problems of handicapped employees, who often have the sympathy of neither management nor their coworkers in their efforts to continue working. Taniguchi san had looked forward to becoming a regular employee in a stable company when she entered Azumi, but as time went on she realized that the conditions she was promised by management in her initial interview were far different from the actual situation, and there was nothing she could do but persist or quit. In her words:

> I entered as a handicapped person, right? So, compared to a regular person, no matter how hard we try, our handicap follows us around like a shadow. It sticks with us, and Azumi, knowing this full well, hired handicapped people. Naturally, if there are times when my legs hurt, well, there will be times like that. At such times, even if I think, "Boy, I sure would like to sit down!" my superiors don't say, "Please go ahead and sit." When I came to Azumi, I had an interview with the people from the personnel department. Then they came right out and said, "If it's tiring, it's OK for you to sit." However, if you say, "Please let me sit" to the people in the place where I was sent to work, they say, "If everybody's standing, how can we let one person sit?" Even if I'm tired, I have to grin and bear the standing up. If only the superiors would have a little more understanding. To all intents and purposes I'm different in every way from the ordinary person, and I wish they'd recognize this point. No matter how much the upper

level people realize this [my immediate superiors don't]. It'd be great if the people in the section would also have this consideration for me. It seems to me that these people at upper levels are not communicating this to the people at the section level.

I asked her if she thought others had similar problems. She said they did and that she wished that all of the handicapped could be put in one workplace, instead of being mainstreamed:

> You see, when they first recruited handicapped people, that's what I thought it was, and that's why I applied. Then I found out I was wrong about that, and without notice I was placed in with regular people. Well, if it's a regular person with dexterous fingers, they can do ten pieces an hour, let's say. For a handicapped person, your legs are bad and your hands aren't able to move well, so naturally you can only do six or seven. There are times when I have doubts how much the bosses really understand this. Even in the newspapers, they wrote it up big that they were recruiting the handicapped. One, two, four people got jobs in I&P. Four entered, two were deaf. The other person and I were the same age, and our legs were equally bad. But naturally they reached the point where they couldn't stand it, and they quit. At first they were pleased. They said, "We've entered a nice place, and if we put up with it here, we can work until retirement." But, in the end, you have times when you're tired, and your legs are bad. It's all right if you can get your point across, but sometimes your point doesn't get across. There's the company's side to it, and the extent of the understanding of the higher-ups. Because of that sort of thing, in the end you can't stand it any more. Finally, all three of them ended up leaving, and now I'm the only one.

How did Taniguchi san manage to survive in spite of these trials? Perhaps she brings her philosophy about her handicap to bear on her attitude toward work as well: "It's no good worrying about it all the time. You have to encourage yourself, I guess you'd say. It's good if you can live with a warm-hearted, light feeling, if you naturally tend toward the bright side. It's no good to feel gloomy. So I bring myself to look at the bright side of things." Moreover, she realized that her parents would not be there to support her forever, and she had to try as hard as she could to keep the job until retirement: "In any case, if I get through to retirement, there's that pension, right? That system is rock solid."

Quitting was not a desirable solution for many. It would mean taking a step down in pay and benefits if one were able to find work at another company as a regular employee, since one would be starting all over again from the bottom of the seniority wage system. Moreover, the chance of finding a job as a regular employee becomes more and more slim as one ages. Thus, if a woman in her forties with over twenty years' of service were to quit, not only would she take a loss in her retirement benefits (see Chap. 4, p. 67), but she would also probably have to settle for a very low-paying job in the peripheral sector as a *paato,* if indeed she had not already exceeded the age limit for that. This is true of male or female employees; those in this stage of their careers are "immobile" employees. Moreover, in the opinion of many people I interviewed, it would be harder for a man at this stage to get any sort of job, especially if he lacked skills.

Azumi was a world away from the British knitting factory where Sallie Westwood (1984) did her fieldwork on women workers. Unlike the "Stitchco" company, where women were highly critical of management and assumed a combative stance, most Azumi women were fairly sympathetic with management and looked within themselves to find ways to cope with the demands of their jobs. If they were at times dissatisfied with management policy, they would complain among themselves; but it rarely went beyond this, and even the most vocal of workers, such as Hasegawa san or Ota san, could hardly be considered militant. A positive attitude toward their work and pride in it were shared by most of the women I knew at Azumi. Some, like Kinami san, were unable to sustain this attitude and ultimately quit. Others are still in the running but do not feel confident that they can last until retirement age.

# 3

# A Lifetime of Line Work: Making It to Sixty

As NOTED in Chapter 1, few Japanese women workers stay on the job to retirement. At Azumi's factory each year roughly 30 percent of the women quit, receiving a lump-sum severance payment.[1] In a nation where lifetime employment in one firm is the ideal, what prevents women from achieving it? The reasons are myriad and complex. I would like to first present a summary of them before dealing with each in more detail. My information comes from conversations with women who were about to quit or contemplated leaving.

Many women still follow the professional housewife model and quit their jobs at marriage. The worker herself may want to concentrate on managing her home, or her in-laws or her own parents may wish her to do so. However, quitting upon marriage is on the decline. As we have seen, many of my coworkers thought that newlyweds should continue working until pregnancy in order to save for the ever-more-costly home. It is still perfectly acceptable, though, for a woman to quit when she marries, although the marriage age is on the rise too.

One factor compelling resignation upon marriage is the woman's job location. Yamamoto san, a twenty-two-year-old in the I&P Section, had an *omiai* (arranged marriage interview) with a man from a distant prefecture. She decided to marry him and quit her job. She did not reach this decision lightly, but was really worried about marrying him. This came out one day when we went shopping for pottery at a bargain sale. She felt she didn't know him well, and she worried that his income as a carpenter in the countryside might not be adequate to support a family. Far from being excited about the new life that lay ahead, she appeared sober and subdued. Living in the countryside would also take some adjustment, and she wasn't sure she would like it. She remarked that working at Azumi with other women day in and day out afforded her little opportunity to meet men and date, and she felt that if she did not marry through *omiai* she would miss out on marriage all together.

Irahara san, a twenty-four-year-old worker at the I&P, was unsure whether or not she would be able to stay on after marriage:

> I can't say. I'm the older of two daughters, so I'm the *atotsugi* [successor]. If things go well and I could get a *mukoyōshi* [husband who agrees to adopt the family name], then I could keep working. But if I marry out, I don't know what circumstances I'd meet with —if it were a place far away, I'd have to quit, or if my husband were transferred, I'd have to quit. If I could, I'd continue at my present job; I don't hate it.

As Irahara san indicates, even if the husband's job is located nearby, it may not remain so. One of the rights large companies reserve in exchange for offering tenured employment is that to transfer regular employees to different branches of the operation over the course of their careers.

Hanami san, a thirty-year-old employee with twelve years of service, resigned when her husband, also a Azumi employee, was transferred to a branch factory far away. Since the company did not give her similar marching orders, she decided to resign and accompany her husband. Far from being bitter about management insensitivity, she said she welcomed the opportunity to concentrate on homemaking and start a family.

Ishimoto san, the only male worker in the I&P, cited the women's own inflexibility about transfer as one of the main drawbacks of keeping them on for the duration:

> We men think it's fine to work until sixty, but maybe it's more difficult for women. Men can transfer anywhere. You can even become *tanshinfunin* [those who live apart from their families because they have been transferred to a branch office]. . . . If the company says, "Well, we'll have you go to a post at X factory," a man can usually accept that. But since a woman has a household,

if she lives here she can't leave, can she? So, even if she doesn't want to, she may have to quit. Women have that problem, don't they? That's difficult. It won't work unless both the individual and the company cooperate, don't you think? . . . Men make a compromise either at work or at home. But I don't think women can do that. There are a lot of women who are making a go of it. Couples where both work. Home and job. But if they do that, they can't work as the company would like them to. Even if they were told, "The Fukushima factory needs this kind of person, and you're fit for it, so you go," a woman couldn't go, could she? A man can be *tanshinfunin,* but not a woman. As the average age of employees keeps on increasing, this becomes more and more a problem.

From the viewpoint of a large company like Azumi, one of the things that makes "lifetime employment" possible is the willingness of their tenured staff to move wherever and whenever business conditions require it. Because men do follow orders to transfer, women's inability to do so reduces management's options in their assignments. Recently, employee transfer has met with criticism due to its deleterious effects on the employees and their families.[2] Some employees have begun to challenge their company's transfer orders. It is possible that the practice will diminish gradually, or at least become more voluntary (Muneto, Fujiwara, Miyaji, and Maekawa 1986).[3] However, as long as it is considered to be part of the natural course of employment, employee transfer is a formidable obstacle to married women workers.[4]

Many women choose to retire at pregnancy or the birth of their first child. The role of the mother is central in Japanese children's upbringing (Lebra 1976), as the Japanese consider the dependency relationship between mother and child to be unique and irreplaceable. Attachment to mother lasts a lifetime, for both males and females. Given the cultural emphasis on this bond, it is not surprising that a woman and/ or her family may desire her to devote herself full time to her infant's development well into childhood.

Other factors may also enter into a woman's decision to resign at pregnancy. Although Article 65 of the Labor Standards Law requires employers to shift pregnant women to lighter work if the women request it, Cook and Hayashi (1980:88) note that many small and medium-sized businesses are not able to accommodate such requests. Apparently large firms, too, find this inconvenient. Azumi's management was not enthusiastic about finding pregnant women in the sewing section more comfortable jobs as they reached the end of their terms. Even if accommodation were made at the workplace, the commute would be a deterrent. If flex-time for pregnant women is not available (it was not at Azumi), rush-hour commuter trains and buses may discourage women from continuing. Employees with a diagnosed risk of miscarriage would usually rather resign than take medical leave and leave their coworkers to make up the slack. Finally, some of those who hold out until after the child is born find they must leave because they cannot find child care.

If the responsibilities of motherhood do not keep a woman from holding on to paid employment, those which come with being a daughter-in-law may. Women are expected to be the primary caretakers of ailing in-laws.[5] If there is no one to look after her own parents, they too may require her help. At Azumi, Kamida *hanchō* foresaw the day when she might have to quit to look after her mother-in-law: "I want to [go on working], but we have Grandma. She's already seventy-three. Grandma's eyes are very bad. She can hardly do any housework, so I do all of it. If Grandma falls down or tires out or goes downhill, I wouldn't be able to work anymore, would I? So depending on that, I want to work as long as I can."

The illness of one's children, too, may either force one to quit or to choose employment as a *paato*. Kushida san, whom we discussed before, came in as a *paato* because she knew she would have to take her child to the clinic on occasion. Shimizu san, a mother of two whose younger son had a heart condition, cited his illness as a contributing factor in her decision to quit her job of seventeen years.

If a woman has stayed on through marriage and pregnancy, has found day care, and is relieved of in-law duty, the next problem may surface when the child enters elementary school. It is sometimes difficult to juggle an elementary schoolchild's schedule with a work schedule. Mothers are expected to attend *sankanbi,* participant-observer days at school, as well as teacher-parent and PTA meetings, which take place during working hours. Moreover, first-graders' school day is only a half-day. If the school system does not have an after-school day-care program, a working mother usually has to arrange for family (usually her in-laws or her parents) or neighbors to care for the child after school. In rare cases, the school system will offer day care. Fujii san confronted this problem when her daughter reached elementary-school age. Since her school district lacked an after-school program, she and her husband decided to sell their house and relocate to a neighboring city where the schools offered after-school day care. Shimizu san, who has one child in elementary school and another who is about to enter first grade, comments:

> I don't plan to work until retirement, because my younger child will enter first grade next year, and with two in school, I'd have to be taking days off or coming to work late too often, which Azumi doesn't allow; it'd cause trouble. Until now, the company has been first in my life, over the household. You can't do fifty-fifty. I saw the company as 70 percent and my family as 30 percent. When the kids get to school age, recently there's been a lot of talk about delinquency and so on, and even though Grandma and Grandpa are at home, I decided to quit Azumi, make the household my central focus, and get a job in the spare time left. Up to now, Grandma had gone to the participant-observer days, or I had taken half-days off. There were times when I myself couldn't go. We did it 50/50. But now, with two kids, that won't work. Plus the children are really happy when their mother goes. And I feel guilty about the fact that until now I've given less attention to the children [than to my job].

Thus, Shimizu san is motivated to quit the job she has held for seventeen years, not only because of the structure of school activities and parental participation in them, but also out of a desire to give more personal attention to her children. She later told me that another factor in her decision to quit was that her husband was due to be transferred in another year or so, and she would have to quit then anyway to accompany him.

Other reasons besides family may lead one to leave the company—for example, a desire to do something else. Murakami san, the *kakari-chō* at the I&P, wants to own a small restaurant someday; Matsumura *hanchō* wishes to become a day-care center employee or a kindergarten teacher. I wonder, though, whether these aren't more dreams than concrete plans. In a return trip in 1990, I learned that both were still plugging away. In Murakami san's case, the restaurant idea may come to fruition after she reaches retirement.

Bad personal relations in the workplace can also force one's hand. This may be connected with any of the previous factors: that is, the company may suggest that a woman's place is in the home and pressure young married women to quit. Or, by making work life unpleasant for those whose production rates have dropped or whose quality control has diminished, the company can effectively force out older workers and those who cannot maintain the pace, as in the case of Kinami san (Chap. 3). In the past, the deliberate hazing of new workers led many young women to quit, according to Kamida *hanchō,* who entered the company in 1962 from junior high school and who has continued to work even after marrying and having children. She noted that there was no one left from her entering group except for two men; all the rest had quit. When I asked why, she replied, "Marriage, because they didn't like the company, and so on." I inquired further, and she explained:

> There used to be a lot of malicious teasing. I cried a lot. Girls are stronger now than they used to be. . . . It was the supervisor—a woman—who was the mean one. Women do that sort of malicious teasing, you know. She yelled at us for brushing against the clothes that were hanging up in the changing room—they didn't have lockers then as we do now. And if you were sewing labels on garments and you asked for some more, she would take a bunch and throw them at you, so they'd fall all over the place, and then you'd have to pick them up. It takes time to pick them up, and then you'd have to rush like crazy to catch up to your quota. I cried a lot. No one would come to help no matter how much I was behind. It was an utter mess. You had to endure it. So I was trained, hardened by that.

Such hazing struck me as counterproductive to efficiency, until I realized that it must have been a very effective method of forcing out less energetic or committed workers. Robert Cole (1971:119) noted that in his Tokyo Diecast plant, "Management tried to screen out incompetents during their trial period before they became regular employees. Once the probation period is past, a number of other devices are available for dealing with regular workers should they become undesirable."

At Azumi, hazing may well have been one of these devices. As Cole found, it is not a simple matter for a company to dismiss a regular employee. (See Chap. 3 for a discussion of dismissal.) This is partly due to the cultural value, shared by management and workers alike, of preserving harmony within the group. Moreover, Azumi employees were confident that the union would guarantee their jobs even if it did not help them in any other way. Perhaps tactics such as hazing were to ensure that those who remained past the first year or so were serious about their work. In relating this story to me, it was obvious that Kamida *hanchō* was proud of having withstood the test, and although she thought some of the teasing had been excessive, she agreed with the premise that one needs to harden oneself in order to work, that work requires commitment. If one's fellow workers take a dim view of one's comportment at work, they too can make life unpleasant by ostracizing and gossiping.

Finally, we cannot forget the *paato,* for whom there is no tenure. Their contracts may be renewed or terminated at the expiration date, depending on the business climate. Kushida san and Mihata san had continued for ten and six years of service respectively, but the company terminated their contracts when it made the decision to move the Inspection and Packaging Section en masse to the shipping center. Production at the factory had been cut, and there was talk that the company would let the number of employees drop as much as possible and turn the factory into a location for the manufacture of trial lots of experimental products only. With highly experienced seamstresses and located near the company's designers at the main office, this urban, domestic factory would suit this purpose well. Moreover, trial products could quickly be tested on the market. When I asked her if she would like to work until the normal retirement age, Kushida san answered: "Hmm . . . if I can, I'd like to. But I wonder . . . if the company has a slowdown. . . ." A few weeks after this interview, her contract was terminated. This is common practice in Japanese companies. Usually the employees who are let go have no recourse but to go out and look for another *paato* job, if they are not already beyond the age limit. When I returned to visit Azumi in 1987, I found that the factory had indeed been downscaled and was producing trial garments only.

As we have seen, many workers entered Azumi because they felt that, as a large and established firm, it would offer employment stability. After two small companies had fallen out from under her, Taniguchi san was thrilled to get her foot in Azumi's door. Will people like her be able to make it to retirement at age sixty and the "rock-solid pension" that awaits them? This is a matter of great consequence, not only for Taniguchi san and those similarly handicapped, but also for all women doing factory work. My coworkers felt that if they could last until fifty-five, the former retirement age, they would be lucky; but now that it has been raised to sixty, they have serious doubts. Previously, as in most Japanese companies, women's retirement age had been fixed at five years earlier than that of men's—fifty rather than fifty-five. This practice of setting differential retirement ages was found by the Supreme Court to be against "good public order" in the 1975 *Izu Cactus Park* lawsuit (Cook and Hayashi 1980:59). The retirement age for both sexes at Azumi subsequently became fifty-five. With the aging of the work force, and the difficulty of finding steady employment at the age of fifty-five, the union pressed the company to extend the retirement age to sixty. The government has also encouraged this extension in recognition of the financial problems of an aging population. Thus, from the standpoint of the government and of the male workers, uniform retirement at age sixty is welcome. The male employee can be assured of his job at a decent wage for an extra five years, whereas previously he would have had to scramble to find other, usually inferior, employment.

For women, too, retirement at sixty is presumably a welcome change. The discriminatory difference between men's and women's ages at retirement has been erased, and now women have an equal chance at that extra five or more (some companies required that women retire ten years earlier than men) years of financial security, depending on the company's policy. This may indeed be so for women in white-collar jobs. But for those whose jobs entail physical dexterity and constant, concentrated use of the eyes, later retirement becomes problematic. The health problem is intensified because the company is intent on raising labor productivity, so that it uses as few employees as possible. Because Azumi has put a virtual freeze on hiring new female employees for factory and shipping-center work, the average age of the employees increases, although the amount of work to be done does not decrease proportionately. Moreover, employees who have quit in recent years have not been replaced. Speed and accuracy are as important as ever, perhaps more so, and exceptions are not made for those who cannot keep up the pace. When I asked if she planned to work until retirement, Ogawa san (age forty-three) replied:

I'm worrying about that now. Actually I'd really like to work.
Now that my kids are big there's no problem with working. But
I'm forty-three now and Azumi's retirement age is fifty-five. I
don't know if I'll be able to work. At least I'd like to make it to
fifty. So I'll try my best over the next seven years. If my health
holds up, I'd like to make it to retirement. But I do inspection—
you use your eyes, and so . . . [I don't know if I'll make it].

She continues: ". . . So when I look at older people who are doing
inspection now, I think if it were me, I couldn't do it. I don't have confidence. I'd like to go on to retirement. But health-wise, physically, I
think it's impossible."

Workers' anxiety about their ability to work to retirement age is
tied to the company's encouragement of older employees to quit well
before then, as well as to the women's feeling that they are causing
inconvenience to their fellow employees when their production rate
slows down, and that they create problems for the company when
their quality control suffers from deteriorating eyesight. Nakanishi
san comments: "It's hard to say [whether I'll work until retirement].
From 1985 the retirement age becomes sixty for both men and
women, right? I think men can make it to sixty, but it's a bit hard for
women. But since it's close [she lives nearby], I want to work as long
as I'm healthy. But I don't know to what extent the company will
allow it." When I asked, "Don't you think it'll be all right?" She
replied, "But if I become a bother to the group it won't do, will it? If I
can work as I do now until sixty, then I want to work, but as you'd
expect, gradually you get worse at remembering, and the hands don't
move well anymore. It won't get any better, will it! But I want to work
as near to retirement as I can, even if it's only one more year."

The types of factory jobs to which women are assigned are generally less varied and therefore more tiring than the jobs of men in similar circumstances. I found this true not only at my company but also at
others—rubber companies, a sign manufacturer, a metal sheeting
manufacturer—which I visited. The assistant department manager at
the shipping center as well as executives at a metal sheeting company
told me that jobs such as inspection and packaging are usually
assigned to women because it would be a waste of money to assign
such tasks to men, whose wages are higher. One reason it would be a
"waste" is that these jobs (including sewing) are also considered to be

particularly suitable to women, who are thought to be more dexterous than men, and who can pay more attention to detail without getting impatient, as men are wont to do. I was told repeatedly by both sexes that women are more suited to such *komakai shigoto* (fine or detailed work).

At Azumi, except for sewing and office work, almost all factory jobs were performed while standing, ostensibly because otherwise it would create an unfair difference between those whose work allowed them to sit and those who had to stand. Moreover, the supervisor explained to me that it looked bad for people to sit down on the job. There were only two breaks, at lunch and at 3:00 P.M. The majority of women workers either stood on concrete floors for most of the day, continuously performing the same actions, or were bent over the sewing machines. When executed continuously over a period of years, this type of work causes an occupational disease called carpal tunnel syndrome. The symptoms involve pain in the tendons and loss of free movement of the arms. Some women also complained of numbness in the arms. There is no remedy for the problem other than to quit the job. Many did find some relief in acupuncture, moxibustion, or plasters sold at any drugstore. Anyone not familiar with the work might think we were hospital out-patients from the sight of these bandage-like plasters stuck on our necks and arms. The company was loath to recognize it as an occupational disease, however, and no woman has yet taken them to task on this problem.

It was generally agreed that sewing was more physically demanding than inspection, packaging, or cutting, so women who could no longer meet the demands of sewing were sometimes shifted to other divisions if there was a place for them. Sewing was particularly a problem for pregnant women, who became too big to sit comfortably at a machine, and for whom the vibration was unpleasant, if not harmful. Some workers told me the reason there were so many miscarriages at the factory was because of the constant use of sewing machines early on in pregnancy, but there was no way to substantiate this claim. The nurses were concerned with the lack of appropriate work for pregnant women, however, and with the company's lack of concern over pregnant women's health.

Most of the work performed by men in the factory consisted of packing and loading boxes for shipment, repairing machines, and performing office and management work. The manual work was performed mainly by two types of employees: mid-career-entry men of low educational attainment, whose pay was low and who had no opportunity to advance within the ranks as did other men, and young college graduates who had recently entered the company and were assigned factory work for a period of one or two years as part of their training in the overall operation. Furthermore, since the company could no longer hire junior high school graduates to perform blue-collar jobs, the most cost-efficient solution was to make a stint in the factory a requisite part of the training process for college graduates. The company no longer hires male high school graduates, because they want employees with access to the promotional track to have the same educational background.

After my research had ended, I learned that the shipping center had instituted a new system whereby women, too, would be handling cartons. Management said the cartons would be made lightweight enough for women to carry with ease (forklifts were not used). This way, women in inspection could themselves be responsible for getting boxes of garments to be inspected and putting away those which were finished. My younger friends were willing to give the new system a try: they saw the handwriting on the wall. The company was pushing for women employees to be more versatile, and they felt it behooved them to make efforts, even if it was *chikara shigoto,* work requiring physical strength. Older women were opposed to the change, however. They complained that lifting boxes made them too tired and gave them backaches. They felt even more the difference in age between them and the younger women who could do the work more easily, and it bothered them that they often had to ask for assistance, thus making nuisances of themselves, whereas the younger women did not. Two of my colleagues in their fifties commented that this box-lifting work meant they would surely have to quit before retirement.

Although loading and shipping are also physically demanding, the jobs allowed for broader and more varied movement, and did not require visual attention to intricate detail. In addition, men were given more leeway regarding the pace of their jobs; if Ishimoto san in I&P Section wanted to sit and have a smoke for a few minutes, no one said a word. The same was true at the shipping center.

Thus, many men who were engaged in manual labor were not going to be doing that work forever, and even those whose jobs would remain the same performed tasks that were, on the whole, less taxing and monotonous. Moreover, possibly because men were not sewing, inspecting, or packaging, they were less subject to demands that they increase pace or meet targets, and so they could occasionally take a moment to sit and relax. I never saw any male employee in the I&P run to and from the restroom as women were told to do.

The retirement age of sixty was looked upon as a boon to the men but as a formidable challenge to the women. Some women felt that this, too, was a ploy on the part of the company to cheat women out of their full retirement payment. Matsumura *hanchō* commented:

> For those in their fifties now, retirement will be at sixty. It's a question of whether or not they can keep going until sixty. If they can't see well, they quit, right? Well, there's truly a big difference in the retirement payment. It's less. When I think about that, I realize what a clever method the company has thought up—they can get by without paying out very much this way [laughs].

I checked with the employee handbook to see if Matsumura *hanchō* was correct in her assessment about the disadvantage of quitting before full retirement. According to the handbook, legitimate reasons for leaving before full retirement are:

1. Death on job or job-related injury/illness which caused retirement.
2. Retirement because of death outside of the workplace.
3. Retirement due to circumstances of the company (beyond worker control).

If one leaves before full retirement for reasons other than the above, the portion of one's retirement payment that takes into account one's grade (in this case, ranking such as "skilled, level no. 1, skilled level no. 2," etc.) is discounted. Only after having worked thirty-one years or more would one receive full benefit, even though one quit before retirement. In the case of a woman who entered the company at age sixteen, she would have to work until age forty-seven before being able to quit without penalty.[6]

Kamida *hanchō* also commented on the difficulties of the new retirement age:

> Even looking at physical strength, there's no comparison between a sixty-year-old woman and a sixty-year-old man, right? I think it's very hard for a woman to work to age sixty. Her ability and

eyesight both get worse, and she just hasn't the freedom of movement. A man aged sixty can still work with vigor. From my viewpoint as a supervisor, with some men it's so, but to think of having a woman work for you until sixty is a headache. You wonder if they can make it. . . . Even if you just have them do inspecting, their efficiency doesn't improve. I guess the limit for women is fifty-five. I think men can work longer, but women's bodies can't cut it.

When Kamida *hanchō* asked me my opinion, I told her I agreed but I thought that the cause lay in the work situation in which women were placed more than any inherent weakness in women as compared to men of the same age. If the company were to give them more variety in their jobs, I suggested, their prospects of making it to retirement would be much improved. Moreover, women have the greater burden of household chores to perform in addition to their work duties, which taxes their strength even more. She said that she had never thought of it in those terms, but that I had a point. Indeed, most of the factory women with whom I discussed this topic had not thought much about the reasons why it was harder for women to reach retirement, beyond the fact that the work became too difficult to perform well. Although they were regular employees who wanted to work until retirement, they did not see this as their entitlement, nor did they complain that they were being unfairly treated in comparison to male employees.

What is the company's position on this issue? The submanager of the personnel department clarified the matter for me one day, during an interview on the pay and promotion system. He was explaining how inappropriate (i.e., costly) the system of *nenkō joretsu* (age-based seniority wage) is for employees who learn simple jobs and then stay in these jobs ad infinitum. In his example:

> For instance, let's say a twenty-year-old in the sewing division gets a monthly pay check of 100,000 yen ($417 @ 240 yen per $1). In her second year, she gets 105,000 yen, and in her third year, so much. When she gets way up here (he points to many years of service), she might make as much as 500,000 yen, right? If it keeps going up and up, even if she's still doing the same sewing, by the time she gets to be fifty . . . what a contradiction, right? If it keeps going up and up, even doing the same job, just by virtue of the *nenkō joretsu*. . . . She is there for thirty years, but her ability

doesn't go up. I doubt if there's much of a difference between that fifty-year-old and a twenty-two-year-old. The eyes get bad, and the hearing goes. It gets hard to read the chits. Even if the ability is there, she becomes handicapped.

Later on in the interview, he commented further on the problem of an aging female work force:

> G: Because, for instance, they can't do the sewing any more?
>
> Y: If her eyes get bad or some such thing, there is no way she can do the work, right? They can't just automatically become independent of their group. If they could, there wouldn't be anything for them to do anyway. The only thing you can do is have them do something, anything, which they are capable of doing. The aging worker has become our biggest problem in every workplace. Take the salesladies. It's no good to have a woman in her fifties selling lingerie! That's straight from the customers' mouths! They really say that. In fact, there really isn't anything which the new Azumi can give these women to do.
>
> G: How about office work?
>
> Y: Only as a last resort. Modern office work, too, can only be handled by young people.
>
> G: You mean computers?
>
> Y: We feel that unless you are in your twenties or thirties, you can't do office work. In Japan today, only such people can do office work. And because they [older women] can't do office work, they go into sales.
>
> G: I see. . . . So what are you going to do about it?
>
> Y: We don't know what to do. We're in trouble. The retirement age becomes sixty next year. Sixty! For everyone.
>
> G: Is that so? From next year?

From this interchange it is obvious that the company never anticipated that women would want to remain at their jobs until retirement; the sorts of jobs assigned women are by definition short-term. The submanager seemed more than a little upset that many women in recent years have stayed on despite marriage and/or pregnancy, and expect to gain the benefits of the *nenkō joretsu* system despite their low status. He is frustrated by the change he sees in women, as became obvious in our next conversation:

You will understand the way women think if you watch their behavior. In the past, one would be thought of as a fool to work in such a place until age sixty. To think of working until sixty! It was only in the exceptional case. Most people used to quit when they got married. Even so, there were a few who wanted to remain. But those people said they'd be glad if only we would keep them on. That was the way they considered it. They figured it wouldn't matter if their monthly wage didn't go up. Most worked with that sort of attitude. But gradually, maybe you could say as the economy developed, [women] started graduating from college, and women's lib entered the scene, and things started moving toward *josei kaihō* [liberation of women]. I guess you could say new problems came up. I guess it's a Japanese problem . . . we have to make some kind of system so that if at forty they can no longer do sales, then at thirty-five they can start training to do office work. If we keep up as we are [the number of] sixty-year-old ladies will double and the company will be in trouble.

Actually, there were no college graduates among the factory workers, and the number of women who even mentioned the phrase *josei kaihō,* or anything like it, was minuscule. However, the economy had a great deal to do with their refusal to quit—they, too, wanted to be homeowners and to give college educations to their children, go on trips, wear nice clothes, and eat out on occasion, as did their better-off neighbors and the ideal families on television, in the movies, and in countless advertisements. Most of my coworkers could not afford such things if they stayed home. They considered them to be important enough to continue working regardless of the problems they encountered. Women who continued working after marriage were becoming increasingly commonplace,[7] and one woman who married and stayed on remarked to another like her that women who quit at marriage are fools, since nowhere could one find a job that paid so well. No one mentioned working out of a desire to be liberated from their families.

In Kamida *hanchō*'s estimation, this is not a temporary trend but one that will continue and for which effective solutions must be sought. She explains:

> Before, when they married they quit right away, or if they got pregnant they'd quit right away, and there were lots of girls that

came right out of school. Moreover, well, you can't exactly call it mechanization, but they've thought of a lot of ways to improve things—methods for speeding up the handling and such. Because they're using methods that allow fewer people to make large quantities of goods, they don't hire as many people. Personnel costs are also quite high, it seems, and as you get older, you can take tests and gradually rise in the ranks; your salary goes up, too. Personnel costs grow high so they cut down on people. If someone says she'll quit, I doubt if they'll try to detain her anymore. To the company, the best thing is for people with high personnel costs to quit, and for cheap young ones to come in. Right now *nobody* is quitting, and as they get older, it gets very difficult to find a job, so even if they think this workplace doesn't come up to their expectations, they put up with it. More and more people are getting to be that way.

She suggested the company would have to find some method of inspection that even older workers could do well, since it did not seem likely that they would quit.

Both the submanager of personnel and Kamida *hanchō* recognize the contradiction between the permanent employment, seniority-based wage system and cultural perspectives on women that view them as short-term workers on whom job training would be wasted. We are again reminded that this system is built on the ideals set forth by Azumi's president in his anniversary speech. Lifetime employment is for men. Who would have expected women to take their jobs so seriously?

Miyazawa san, a nurse in Azumi's Health Section, offered some insights on women workers' problems in remaining until retirement. It was her opinion that the company did not actually want women employees to stay on, and this naturally affected their treatment. I asked her if this was true of office as well as factory workers. She replied:

Yes, they are the same. They prefer young people. They're making a woman's product and selling it to women. Those making the product are women, and those who sell it in the end are women, at the department stores and boutiques. But there's little feeling for trying to improve things for these people. People think that Azumi must be great, that since it's a women's company the treatment of female employees must be wonderful; but if you compare it to Nihon Denshi it's not good at all. I've talked to women who work there, and even in their thirties and forties, they don't feel as if they've worn out their welcome [*izurai to iu ki wa shinai*]. But here, when you pass thirty—or if you're doing office work, twenty-five—it inevitably becomes hard to stay on. Even women with some skills feel that the company wants them to quit when they reach forty. There's no feeling that it's only natural that they should feel at ease being there. I'm dissatisfied about that. Even I was told by the submanager of the personnel department, "Just as you'd expect, women with kids are out a lot, aren't they. . . ." [This comment was directed toward Miyazawa herself, who has children.] I think however you look at it, it's hard for women to work.

She then adds that even for certain male employees, continuing in their careers is not unproblematic:

Moreover, even for men, if they're weak—if they get sick or are out sick for months, or if they have something chronic, they can't be as active in their work as the ordinary people. They can't go out on business *(shutchō)*, or they can't do overtime. They have a handicap vis-à-vis other employees. When it comes to climbing the ladder, if you once make a wrong step, unless you have exceptional ability, you lose in comparison with the ordinary [healthier] employee.

From conversations with the nurses, with the *kachō* of the health management section, and with the employees themselves, I reached the conclusion that Azumi was not progressive in the realm of employee health and fitness, especially the factory employees. Whereas main office workers had a brighter environment, a more relaxed pace, and offered aerobics classes after work for whoever cared to join, factory employees had none of these benefits. Of course, one could say that no factory is ever going to be as comfortable a place to work as an office, but there were many ways in which the factory worker's environment could have been improved without too much additional investment of funds. From Miyazawa san's comment above, one could also infer that blue- and white-collar workers alike have problems if they become unable to work at the level expected of them.

Although Lock (1980) indicated that Japanese companies are concerned about their employees' health and extremely generous with sick leaves, offering up to six months with pay, Azumi was not so benevolent. Lock (1980:82) states: "It is noteworthy that many company employees in Japan do not take their allotted vacation from work, because of their sense of dedication, and that these same men take all their annual sick leave because only thus can they rest and recuperate without a sense of guilt." Lock's analysis was based on interviews with doctors, whose reference group was male, regular employees. My analysis, in contrast, is based on conversations with nurses from Azumi, who were responding to my queries about women workers in whom the company had invested little training. This may well explain the discrepancy between our observations (conversation with Margaret Lock, July 1989). Making it difficult for these women to take sick leave no doubt led to more employees quitting before retirement—a desirable outcome from management's viewpoint. It is likely that Azumi's weakening financial position at this time also played a part in the company's disregard for the suggestions of its health section staff. While many of Azumi's women did not take personal paid holidays, it was not for lack of wanting to, as we shall see.

# 4

# *Time Off*

UNLIKE blue-collar workers in many industrialized countries, Azumi's blue collars were salaried employees. Under the policy of *sōgo shinrai* (mutual trust), instituted at the time of unionization in 1962, all employees were allowed to be up to a half-day late or leave a half-day early from work without losing any of their monthly salary. They did not punch a time clock. This policy was not, however, an indication of a relaxed attitude toward absenteeism on the part of management. Indeed, Azumi management personnel identified tardiness and absenteeism as a major problem among my coworkers. They tried very hard to keep absentee rates low. Prominent among them was Murakami *kakarichō*.

At the I&P, if an employee was sick or for any other reason had taken the previous day off, s/he had to offer the group an apology at the morning ceremony. The most common was, "I'm sorry for having caused you trouble by selfishly taking the whole day off yesterday when all of you were so busy," or some variation thereof. This, like the *hansei* practice, was peculiar to Murakami *kakarichō* and to my knowledge was not practiced in other parts of the company. Whereas *hansei* signaled the importance of quality control, apology over absence pointed to the problem of maintaining production levels while faced with a personnel deficit. As a manager, Murakami san apparently felt that these issues could be dealt with by calling on her employees to put their integrity on the line to overcome the problems.

On paper, all Azumi employees were entitled to a certain number of paid personal holidays to be taken at the discretion of the employee. These were distinguished from paid national holidays and the company holidays at midsummer and the new year. When I first heard someone apologize for being absent, I wondered how easy it was for people to take days off if it required such a display for each offense, as it were. At least in my mind, apologies are associated with assessment of fault and acknowledgment of wrongdoing. Did these employees feel that they had violated some code by their absence? If so, what code? Or was it a ploy on the part of the *kakarichō* to make it more difficult to take time off? Were the employees, then, insincere in their apologies? Indeed, does sincerity matter, or is this a *tatemae*[1] matter, wherein the employee reaffirms indebtedness to the company and her coworkers: in other words, more an expression of solidarity with the group than culpability in taking a day off? Wagatsuma and Rossett (1986) demonstrate the importance of apology in Japan as a restorative act more than a deeply felt admission of guilt. In this case, the employee, by apologizing, would be acknowledging her indebtedness to her coworkers, her submission to the company, and her willingness to cooperate in the future. Whether or not she actually felt culpability in taking a holiday would be irrelevant. Unlike in Western culture, *honne* and *tatemae* need not be congruent for the apology to be "genuine." As Wagatsuma and Rossett (1986:473) put it:

> . . . The act of apologizing can be significant for its own sake as an acknowledgment of the authority of the hierarchical structure upon which social harmony is based. At a deeper psychological level, the restoration of a harmonious relationship is attained by the denying of self-serving and self-preserving tendencies. In this context, the external act of apology becomes significant as an act of self-denigration and submission, which of itself is the important message. Thus the internal state of mind of the person who tenders the apology is of less concern.

The issue is in fact complex. It was extremely difficult for employees to take their paid holidays, especially at the factory. This topic came up many times in the interviews. Even the *paato* said it was hard to take a day off. As a general rule, *paato* are by definition not expected to have the same commitment to the firm as regular employees; they may adjust their hours much more easily than regulars (Kondo 1983). In the case of Murakami *kakarichō* and the I&P, I would say that having her subordinates apologize for their absences was a method of impressing upon them the fact that one's absence inconveniences others. Everyone understood that when someone takes an occasional day off, it means that much extra work for everyone else. If personal relations are to go smoothly, one must strive not to cause trouble for others, for otherwise it would become difficult to continue working. Thus the employees were sincere in their apologies, but more out of feeling for their fellow employees than out of loyalty to a company whose aim was zero absenteeism. Hasegawa san gives a vivid example of the problem:

> H: . . . I don't know about the shipping center since I haven't taken a paid holiday yet, but at the factory, if you thought you wanted one day you'd have to ask three months in advance, and even so it was hard to get. Let's say you want to go on a trip so you ask for the day. There's a Saturday and Sunday off, and you want one more day. They won't give it to you. I got into a fight over it once, when Usui was the *hanchō*. Murakami made her refuse and I fought. When I asked, "What, then, are personal paid leaves *for*?" They said, "They're for sickness or weddings or funerals or such times." So I had a terrible fight.
>
> G: With Usui?
>
> H: Yes. Murakami is clever, so she says nothing herself. She gets the *hanchō* to say it, and runs away. I had an awful argument just to get that one day off. Even though I asked three months in advance, I couldn't get it.
>
> G: What happened in the end?
>
> H: I got it. I fought and fought. And finally I got the one day. They said it was in exchange for a sick day, but I said I'd have none of that. I said since it's something that is legally given to workers, it's up to the individual to decide how she wants to use it. Imagine! Saying it was in exchange for being sick! At that time there was the general morning gathering on the first of every month. Then they would announce the attendance rates—who got first place, who got second, and so on. They said, "Inspection and Packaging got 100 percent this month!" and then they'd give some kind of present for it. It's because they want the 100 percent that they won't give you a day off. And if you ask whether the higher-ups don't take days off, well . . . they take a holiday and even go on trips! Murakami went on a long trip with her lover to

Port Pier [in Kobe], telling us all to do overtime! We were all busy, doing overtime. Yes! Everybody was so mad at her afterward, although she didn't know it—we kept it a secret. Yes—if we wanted one day off we had to explain it to the last detail. But some things you just can't bring yourself to say. . . .

G: But you sure hung in there. And you finally got your day.

H: Yes, I finally got it. I sure fought.

G: Did others fight?

H: No, they didn't, and they didn't get many days off, either. I argued because I said, "It's because I'm going on a trip." I said it in a loud voice during work. I argued in a loud voice. Very loud. I argued all day and in the end I felt like I didn't want it after all. But the people who did that got the holidays. Boy, did I fight to get that day! If you wanted to use a personal day you could only do it once or twice a year. But even for those one or two days, you could only use them if you were sick. Not for trips. This was the first time in ten years I'd used one for a trip. And I quarreled like that to get it. Thus, the higher-ups think that I fight over anything, right away. Well, I always do. I never keep quiet and simmer when somebody yells at me. If I'm yelled at, I give it back.

G: I guess that's the best way.

H: It's no good to just leave it with their having yelled at you. If you're yelled at, they'll say something wrongheaded again. So I speak out. That's why the superiors get mad.

Hasegawa san fought for her right to take a day off, but she was also always very careful about personal relationships. At the shipping center, even when it was no longer a rule to apologize for one's absence, she still did so individually to the workers in her group. She asserted her rights, but she knew there was more than this to maintaining a positive working environment. Hasegawa san often complained to me when she thought the company was treating employees unfairly; another case, which I shall discuss later, was that of her objections to the pay scale. She had a clear idea of what she considered her rights vis-à-vis the company.

This attitude was more the exception than the rule, for more often than not my coworkers failed to realize that their complaints could be justified legally and that the company's treatment was not in strict accordance with the law. Whether or not they felt they were being

unjustly treated, they knew that there was no reliable avenue for grievance, that no place else would be any better, and that the bottom line
was to comply or quit. More often than not, my fellow employees
endured Murakami san's double standards in silence. In Lebra's terms,
this is a form of "nonconfrontational conflict management (Krauss et
al. 1984:54). She explains, "Instead of rejecting or correcting an undesirable state of affairs, the individual persuades himself or is advised
by someone to accept it." She further comments that in Japanese
Morita psychotherapy, "acceptance of one's stress or conflict is facili-
tated by the realization that similar problems are shared by others"
(1984:55). Certainly Azumi's women took comfort in the realization
that all had common problems at work. They often mentioned this
when making their complaints in private. This attitude makes it all the
more difficult for an employee to bring a grievance into the open, as
Hasegawa san did. In so doing she was opening herself up to criticism
from those who suffered in silence. Although forbearance and endur-
ance are admirable qualities in both men and women, my impression
is that women, more than men, are expected to display these strengths
more consistently. Azumi's company president indicated this when he
spoke of women's spiritual strength, which remains intact even when
men's falters. He did not mention the effect on their blood pressure.

Hasegawa san's success in bucking the system was based on her
strong record of achievement with the company combined with her
sense of justice and her spunk. These factors gave her an advantage
over others, who tried to negotiate holidays and ended up taking half-
days or falsely claimed illness. The latter course of action was risky,
however, since if an employee called in sick, the automatic response
was to ask her to go to the doctor's office for an examination and call
in again with the results.

Where did the supervisor stand on this issue? Usui *hanchō* happened to bring up the topic in her discussion of differences between
male and female superiors. She said that men are quick to act but
women get caught up in details, which can put them at a disadvantage. When I asked her if that described her own behavior as a *hanchō*
as well, she said it did, and the example she gave was that of how to
handle situations where employees ask for time off:

> U: In the case of a man [supervisor], if someone said, "I'm sorry
> but I'd like a day off," he'd say, "Yes, yes," and that would be it.

But being a woman, I had to ask why, even though I'd been in her position before. I felt uneasy at having to go so far to pin the person down, since it's vacation time that's every person's due. I felt this contradiction even while questioning her. But I didn't have the inner strength to stop myself. But to a certain extent I was flexible, and gave the person a day off on my own responsibility.

G: What do you do if the person refuses to give a reason why they want to take a day off?

U: That usually doesn't happen. Maybe it's because I'm easy to talk to, but they usually come saying that for such and such reason they'd like the time off, although it must seem unreasonable, but could I do something about it for them. So I go with them to the *kakarichō* to talk it over. Then I tell the *kakarichō* that I wish the worker would give in a bit more, but I simultaneously offer to manage somehow to cover for her, so please to give her the time off. But I don't do this for people who are chronically absent. I force them to come [to work].

Even the *hanchō* had mixed feelings about making it so difficult for employees to take a vacation which is their due. What is particularly interesting is that she blames her inability simply to accede to such requests on the fact that she is a woman as much as on the company preference that employees not take holidays. According to her reasoning, because she is a woman, she feels compelled to find out why the vacation is desired; if she were a man, she would not bother to ask. Indeed, most of the women I interviewed said that it is easier to work for a man because women are so picky about unimportant matters. (See Chapter 6, on personal relationships.)

Of course, the self-imposed shortage of employees is the major factor in the company's reluctance to permit employees to take personal holidays. The I&P was particularly short-handed, as the possibilities for automation were limited and the employees took their tenure seriously, unlike the expanding sales staff. Usui *hanchō* further comments:

Speaking about rank, *hanchō* want vacations the same as others do. But since the orders come down from above, it's useless. You want to give them a day off. You want to give it to them. But if you do, then there's one day's work down the drain. And if that day's-worth of work can't get done, your superior will ask you

"Why?"—and it's not good to be asked that, right? Therefore I tell the people below me to take a half-day off rather than a full one. Within the limits of adaptability—if it was absolutely necessary, I could exaggerate (the excuse to the *kakarichō*) and give her the day off.

Besides the employee shortage, another factor contributing to the difficulty of taking holidays in I&P Section was the philosophy of the *kakarichō,* who told me that life consists of "study and effort until you die." She said she did not believe in taking long vacations because they are not good for the brain. While most would disagree with Mura-kami *kakarichō* about the deleterious effects of vacations, many would undoubtedly agree on the importance of study and effort in life. Rohlen (1992:328) sees the roots of this attitude toward learning in Japan's heritage of Confucian values. As he states, in the Confucian tradition, ". . . self-cultivation through the disciplined pursuit of knowledge is the path to human perfection. . . . Self-development is a lifelong opportunity, and since wisdom grows with experience and study, age, knowledge, and authority are positively correlated in the Confucian conception."[2]

At the shipping center where the work atmosphere was relaxed in comparison to the I&P, it was still no easy feat to obtain a day off. Matsumura *hanchō* tried as hard as possible to get the employee to take only a half-day, on the grounds that pay would not be docked, and at year's end she could redeem these untaken holidays in cash. She also felt that just because there is a regulation entitling employees to a certain number of paid holidays does not mean that the employee should take a legalistic attitude and insist on her right to take them. Rather, one should work in good faith and take time off only when absolutely necessary. Without that attitude, the workplace would be devoid of warmth and some employees might lose their jobs. Her meaning is not clear here, but I think she is referring to the fact that if people take vacations casually, those who remain at work have to shoulder the extra burden, since there is no one to cover for absentees. Eventually this would have a deleterious effect on production, and that would lead to a less stable work environment, especially for those with lower achievement records. Her reply also demonstrates the well-known Japanese preference to depend on the compassion of one's fel-lows—a "wet" relationship—rather than on the "dry" relationship where a written contract mediates between people.[3] The topic came up when I asked her about the dangers of abolishing the present restrictions on overtime for women:

> G: Don't you think that if there's no law some companies may force people to do overtime?
>
> M: They have to respect people's wishes. If they leave it up to each person rather than having a standard, then there is no special regulation. Now, because there is a standard, everyone is spoiled by it. If they [employees] are calculating about it, it ends up being a workplace devoid of warmth just because of that. Even if you don't own the company. You should cooperate and work. If we could get people to feel that way, I think that everyone could work. But if they work with the feeling that as long as they just put in their time until retirement they can get paid—that is totally impossible. Instead of saying, "Today I have business to take care of so give me the day off," I think it's better to say, "Today I have business to take care of, so I'll be a little late for work, but I will come."

Although every employee needs an occasional day off, the problem is particularly acute for mothers of small children. Women who needed to attend school functions could usually manage by taking only a half-day, but if the child was sick, this often became impossible. When I asked Ota san how Azumi could be made a better workplace, she answered:

> Freely take paid personal leave, to relax the body and soul. For instance, many of these girls have children and are in dual-worker families. But if the child gets a fever, they can't go home unless they make a big production out of it [*enryoshite, enryoshite*].[4] They must tell the *hanchō,* then the *kakarichō,* then say goodbye to the *kachō* before going home. It's a very difficult position to be in. Even if they know the child has a fever of 39 degrees [Centigrade] it takes an hour before you can go home. If you get a call from home, you should be able to leave then and there with no hassle. If only they didn't make it such a place to work! As a place for women to work to retirement, I think it's a very difficult company to work for.

When I asked Ota san what she did when *her* children were sick, she replied:

I talk it over right away with my parents and decide which is more necessary—to stay at work or go home. If I think my child is more important, I go home, no matter what they may tell me—that's the position I take. So, in my case, I make up my mind which is more important. If the child just has a cold but I have things that must be done at work, I choose work. If the child needs me more, I arrange to leave early, no matter what they think. That's been my experience up to now. I wouldn't be able to continue if I didn't do it that way.

Obviously, Ota san is committed to her job and realizes she cannot be cavalier about being absent. Nonetheless, there are times when she has had to be absent to care for her child, and at such times the company's stance only adds to her difficulties as a woman worker. Ota san managed to stay on because she makes her decisions and stands firm, without regrets. This attitude was an asset for women determined to remain at Azumi.

Many of my coworkers who had small children lived with relatives, or close to them, and asked their husbands' mothers or their own mothers to look after the children if they were ill. Koga san, whose mother lives nearby, remarked:

> K: I stay home from work and take care of them.
> G: Is that OK with the company?
> K: I think the first one or two days is OK. But gradually. . . .

So I have Grandma or someone look after them. My mother. In the cases when you absolutely shouldn't move them, those times when fever developed, I had to take them to the doctor, or even Grandma took them. In those cases I took time off. Even three or four days, because there was nothing else I could do.

Usui san's situation was similar: "If they have a high fever I take them to the hospital. But if it's not so serious, my mother-in-law takes care of them. When I can't go to the hospital because of work, I almost always leave the kids at my parent's home with my younger sister. I take them by car and drop them off, and she'll take them to the hospital for me."

Kamida *hanchō,* who lived with her mother-in-law, always had a built-in babysitter. Still, she did stay home if the illness was serious: "When it was really bad I took off from work, but naturally if you're working you can't make up all sorts of excuses. I was definite about that. If it wasn't anything serious, I'd ask Grandma to please take care of the situation for me, and I'd go to work. You can't take much time off, right?"

Two other workers who did not have relatives they could depend on to care for their children sometimes took turns with their husbands. I was rather surprised to hear this, since in a society where child care is considered to be women's work, I had thought it would be even more difficult for fathers than for mothers to take days off to care for sick children. However, this was not necessarily the case. Fujii san, whose husband worked in a local factory, said:

> F: Do I stay away from work, you mean? I have my husband stay home. Or I have my mother look after them.
> G: Your mother doesn't work?
> F: No, she's at home.
> G: Why does your husband take time off from work?
> F: It's easier to take off at his workplace. It's hard to take time off at Azumi. At my husband's place, he can get a day off right away, so I have him stay home.

Nishitani san, whose husband worked as a manager at a local factory, said: "I take the day off if I have to, but if it's inconvenient with the company, I ask my husband to. And if neither of us is able to easily, we choose whoever is more flexible."

Their husbands' companies' attitude toward workers taking time off is probably not the only reason that these two women's husbands cooperate. These men also seemed particularly willing to help around the home, an unusual trait.

The company was quite clear about its attitude toward absences, and the workers, realizing this, did their best to avoid causing the company any inconvenience. Yet I was told frequently by management how difficult it is when mothers with small children are late to work or have to be absent. The general consensus of management was that such mothers would do the company and their families a favor by quitting their jobs and staying at home. This sentiment was made explicit, in fact. Nakanishi san told me that twice in the past four years the head of the shipping center had made speeches at the morning ceremony telling the workers that the first years of a child's life are the most precious, and if they could possibly manage it they should stay home with their babies at that time. She said everyone thought he was way off-base when so many in the room were mothers of toddlers. The problem of taking personal paid holidays could be analyzed in Sally Falk Moore's (Moore 1975) terms of the semiautonomous field —social groups that generate and enforce norms. The Labor Standards Law and the new constitution and civil code were part of the legal reforms forced upon the Japanese by the American Occupation Forces in 1947 with the intent of democratizing the nation's social and political institutions. However, due to gaps between Japanese custom and the behavior stipulated in the new legislation, it has taken many years for people to make use of the law to change situations still influenced by prewar custom. The Labor Standards Law exists in principle, but Japanese companies have their own "corporate culture," which, for instance, informally dictates that women quit upon marriage or childbirth, or that one should not take one's personal paid holidays, or that employees should not press to have lighter work during pregnancy, and so on. Depending on the company, and within the company depending on each supervisor's interpretation of corporate culture, actual shop conditions may be closer to or further away from those stipulated in the Labor Standards Law.

We might ask whether the I&P was an exception in a factory where a generally relaxed policy on personal paid holidays prevailed. In a survey on child-care strategies, I included a question about the ease of taking a day off when a child was ill, but the personnel submanager blue-penciled it before he would grant permission to distribute the survey. This in itself spoke volumes about the sensitivity of the issue. Azumi is certainly not alone in discouraging employees from taking holidays, however. In 1984, the New Japan Women's Association surveyed women workers about work and health (*Shin Nihon Fujin no Kai* 1985:46–47).[5] The 5,731 respondents were members and their coworkers. Of the respondents, 16.2 percent reported they could take personal paid holidays anytime, and 48.4 percent could take them fairly easily; 27.6 percent took them with difficulty, and 2.7 percent could not take them at all. Of the latter two groups, the reasons most cited were "Because we are busy" (68.5 percent) and "If I take off, it will inconvenience others" (66.5 percent). An additional 21.2 percent said that their bosses would not take kindly to it, and 20.4 percent said, "Because others do not take vacations." One thing to note is the importance of other workers' opinions. Certainly the company sets the baseline for the difficulty of taking one's holidays, but after this, concern about colleagues compounds it.

Within the corporation, it is extremely difficult for a worker to force the company to conform to the law. This may be true anywhere. At Azumi, some workers agree with the company and see their policies as just. Others passively accept the situation but complain in private. A third group usually puts up with conditions but occasionally makes open protest. Last and fewest are those who actively disapprove and try to form groups and educate others to change the corporate culture to conform to the law. The only formal structure that ostensibly acts to improve labor conditions is the union, but it, too, is greatly influenced by the corporate culture and is mindful of the competitive status of the company.

Conformity does not necessarily indicate consensus, however. As Mouer (1986) demonstrates, the road to social harmony in Japan is paved with elaborate social controls. In his words, "Some people may still want to confront authority even after there is a noose around their necks, but one yank on the rope will usually straighten them out and put them in their place" (1986:267). The price my coworkers would pay for consistently and stubbornly resisting the informal rules of company life is *katatataki* (a tap on the shoulder). Ultimately they would find themselves jobless, and they know it.

A very few employees do use the law to challenge corporate policy. For instance, one of my coworkers became pregnant and learned that she was in danger of miscarrying. Rather than retire from Azumi, she took the unprecedented step of filing for medical leave. She later returned to work after the baby was born and the ordinary maternity leave had expired.

By taking the medical leave, this woman was pushing her group of coworkers to the limits of what they considered a responsible employee owed the company. They were quite surprised that she would proclaim it her "right" and actually file the claim. Some said they thought it was going too far. Ultimately, their disapproval of her action was not so much because it defied company policy but because of her failure to fulfill her obligations to her network of coworkers. During her absence she never showed her face at the shipping center to express her regret at causing everyone so much inconvenience and her appreciation for their efforts to fill in for her. Her lack of concern for her coworkers made them feel that her action was unethical, legality aside. As Lebra (Krauss et al., 1984:56) observes, "The unrestrained pursuit of one's own interest at the expense of another's goes against the norm of sociability." Thus there is more than one layer of custom with which the employee who wishes to defy company policy must contend.

Finally, I should note that my impression was that, observations of management notwithstanding, to me tardiness and absenteeism among my coworkers was very low. I did not have access to absenteeism records, unfortunately, so I cannot say definitively how male and female workers compared on that score. It could be that the managers were counting maternity leave and child-care time as a form of absenteeism.

This chapter has delineated another set of reasons why a woman might want to quit her Azumi job. It was certainly no place for shirkers, nor would it suit someone without an adequate family support system. Why did these women continue to work at Azumi? What did they enjoy about their jobs? Could one make a meaningful career out of a factory job at Azumi?

# 5

# *Enjoying Azumi: Building Careers*

LIFE AS an Azumi employee was tough. The work was tiring, especially at the Inspection and Packaging Section, as Murakami *kakarichō* was a hard taskmistress. During the interviews I asked my coworkers what, if anything, they liked about their jobs.

Answers ranged from "nothing special," to pleasure at seeing the new product styles, to enjoyment of the sewing involved, to the cleanliness of the work, to its personal challenge. Oddly enough, the woman who most strongly responded "nothing special" was one who had been in authority, Tahara *kakarichō:* "What do I like most? There isn't really anything. . . . I do it just because I have to. . . . It's not that I like it in particular." Tahara san had already reached the end of her career at Azumi, had formally retired, and was at this point kept on as a *shokutaku*[1] working in the I&P Section as an inspector with the rest of the unranked employees. This loss of status was difficult for her in many ways, and probably contributed to her response.

I would surmise that the men who comprise most *shokutaku* would give similar answers. In Tahara san's case, the management indicated to me that they had let her stay on as a special favor for her years of loyal service. Moreover, the retirement age for women changed from fifty to fifty-five just as she was about to retire, so it was arranged that she would remain at work until fifty-five, but not as a regular employee.

Interestingly enough, Murakami *kakarichō* also said that there was nothing special that appealed to her about her work. This is perhaps because she, too, felt that she had reached her limits at the company. She said she was good at managing people but was not capable of business management, so she did not plan to take any more tests for promotion. Moreover, the group for which she had been responsible for the past several years had been recently disbanded, and at the time of the interview she was doing work to which she was unaccustomed, and which she said was difficult for her. Indeed, she was considering leaving to start her own small restaurant.

Others had something positive to say, even if the praise was faint. Ogawa san replied: "It's clean work. I like that. But there's nothing else that especially appeals to me. Because it's clean work, it's a workplace that women want to work at—if you say "Azumi." . . . So I take pride in working here."

Ogawa san was not alone in her pride in the company. My coworkers often praised the company products, and would not think of wearing any other brand of lingerie. In fact, there was one woman who was in disfavor with practically everyone in the division, and one of the scornful rumors about her was that she even wore "Brand X" apparel. Probably not coincidentally, she also was a midentry employee, having come from a rival lingerie firm.

Another answer along similar lines was that of Nakada san, who was packaging leotards for shipment. She commented: "Nothing special, but I like to see all the new products before other people get to see them, and try them out, and recommend them to people and explain them. It's fun to look at the products, too—the variety of leotards, and so on."

## Challenge

Others were more unreservedly positive. This attitude was not necessarily limited to those having some degree of autonomy in and control over their work; Hasegawa san, who was in inspection work, a highly repetitive and tiring job, saw it as a challenge: "Any work is hard. But I like whatever is given to me. If it's inspection, I work with a target, trying not to let anyone else beat me. I like work—any kind of work."

In fact, when the people from the I&P Section moved to the shipping center, one of Hasegawa san's complaints about work there was that it was done in a group, with group targets, so that individuals could not measure themselves against others; nor could they fix responsibility if someone made a mistake:

> The factory was strict. Very. But we did do work with a target in mind, so I liked the factory better than the shipping center, as far as work content goes. Now, if a defective piece is found, you don't know whose fault it is at all. And we don't have targets as such. We don't even know how many each person completed. You get slipshod. For me, it's better to have a target and work along with it in mind. . . . If one person can do a lot, then you try hard, thinking not to lose to her, right? I like that way better. I like the shipping center, but I guess even if it's hard, I prefer having a target while doing work, like at the factory. . . . No matter what company it is, there are both good and bad aspects. It's not all good. You just have to be patient.

Ishimoto san, the only male in the I&P Section, also complained that work is difficult without someone to measure yourself against. He wanted someone by his side doing similar work, so that they could point out each other's mistakes and keep each other on their toes. The presence of a colleague would also give the supervisor grounds for comparison when it came time for evaluations for bonuses, he thought.

At the I&P, the lack of a target was a problem for people who were not doing inspection. One morning at the PC (Production Control) meeting of our packaging group, Kushida san said that she thought our group should have targets when we did spot-check inspections, just as the regular inspectors did. The problem was that our group was left with empty hands when there was nothing to be packaged, and at such times we were supposed to reinspect items that the inspection groups had already processed. Whereas I tended to look upon such lulls as a welcome change of pace, and as a chance to be free of the ominous *mokuhyō* (targets), she apparently saw them as boring intervals, lacking challenge: "There isn't much work now. You don't know what to do. Most of our work now is spot-check inspection. It's not so good. You have to try your best at spot-checks, too, but . . . somehow, I wish I had my own work to do. If I had a lot of work, I think I could handle it, and it'd be worth doing. I don't like having my hands empty."

Moreover, the fact that we packagers were often less busy than the inspectors, although we were in the same division, caused strains in personal relationships. Ogawa san mentioned that she thought it unfair for work to be so much harder for some than others in the same section. A desire to rectify this discrepancy could have been part of the motivation for Kushida san's suggestion.

## Autonomy

Other workers also said what they liked most about their jobs was that they provided some sense of accomplishment and allowed them some autonomy. Nishitani san, leader of a group in selective inspection and shipping, commented: "I am allowed to do the work as I please. It's left up to me. I can give my opinions. I have autonomy. It suits my personality. There isn't anyone telling me what to do all the time. I say what to do, and I do it." Nishitani san had also had experience as a member of a large group in which she exercised no authority; I asked her to compare it to her present job. She said:

> I can't stand being pushed around from above when I don't know anything that's going on and I'm below. There is an appeal in work that you can complete by yourself, and others acknowledge you for it. But there is no appeal in work that you complete when you do it with everyone together. I don't like that sort of work much. I want them to give me individual responsibility. When you're all together, you get spoiled. When I first came, it seemed good to be in a group in case you made a mistake, but . . . I prefer to be by myself rather than in a group . . . and have them recognize the work as my accomplishment. That's the most satisfying for me.

Ota san, too, liked having a great deal of responsibility in her work. Her job was in materials ordering and handling, and she had to negotiate shipment dates with the material suppliers. She comments: "If I were to mess up, the factory would stop. So the work has meaning— it's worth doing [*yarigai ga aru*]."

## Careers: Four Cameos

Some of the women who had been at Azumi for years had interesting stories to tell about their experiences. Those who had been promoted to supervisory positions gave some of the richest accounts of how they had managed within the system. Here are the careers of four of Azumi's "survivors."

## USUI HANCHŌ

Usui *hanchō*, whom I mentioned previously, works at the factory supervising its dealings with the subcontractor. She entered Azumi in 1968, straight from junior high school. She decided on this company because she liked to make things and was in a sewing club at school. She came to the factory on an observation trip and liked it because it was so clean and pretty. Although two of her friends joined the company at the same time, they ended up quitting after two or three years because they lacked sufficient interest in the work to do well. Usui feels that she has been able to continue so long because she is really interested in sewing.

She did sewing for her first eight years. At some point she was made *shisutaa*, although she did not say when. When she went to the I&P Section at age twenty-three or twenty-four, she became *hanchō*. This was also the time when she married. When I asked her if before marriage she had planned to remain at work after marriage, she replied:

> No. (laughs). I yearned for retirement at marriage. But just when I got married was when I really got into being a *hanchō*—the work began to appeal to me. Before that I thought I'd definitely quit if I got married. But since I started really enjoying the work, I thought I'd quit when I got pregnant instead. But even when I got pregnant, I felt after all that this work really suits me, so I couldn't quit.

Marriage, the responsibilities of being *hanchō* of a new division, and pregnancy all came quickly. Usui san had her first child at twenty-six, her second at twenty-eight. She continued her job as before, still doing overtime and refusing to take the two years' of child-care time:[2]

> U: I have a rather strong sense of responsibility. Even right after having my children, I did overtime. Also, I didn't take child-care time for either child. Together it would have been four years, but I never took one day.
>
> G: Because you were *hanchō*?
>
> U: When you're a *hanchō*, you can't take it. They didn't ask me

not to take it, but I knew how terrible it would be being *hanchō,* having the responsibility—to take an hour off. When I was pregnant, too, I did overtime quite a bit.

G: Weren't you tired?

U: Yes, but there was nothing to be done about it. When I was *hanchō* I didn't feel any particular contradiction in doing overtime, but since coming to production, I've been dissatisfied with the overtime we have to do as a result of late samples or late materials, because during normal hours we have idle hands. If you make the delivery date clear, and materials arrive on schedule, then overtime is unnecessary. But if materials aren't together, or you have that sort of trouble, then you end up having to do overtime almost every day. I was pretty much able to do overtime because I had the understanding of my mother-in-law, who would look after the kids for me, or my husband, who could pick them up for me. But some people can't do that, and even so, I sometimes had to make them do it. So overtime on account of late materials was a big headache.

Usui san made all these sacrifices for a post that provided her with a 3,000-yen-per-month allowance in recompense for her extra duties. In 1983, at the exchange rate of 240 yen to the dollar, this was about US $12.00. One would think that the job must have been especially enjoyable. Yet listening to her account of the first few years of being a *hanchō* under Murakami *kakarichō,* it is difficult to conclude so:

At first it was OK, but the worst time lasted for two years, and within that, one year especially was bad. The problem was that when I became *hanchō* I was put in charge of a kind of work with which I was unfamiliar, and the people underneath me knew more about it than I did. They asked me question after question. So I lost my ability to think, in such a position. I felt I couldn't do it myself. So for half a year I kept telling Murakami that I'd like to quit the job [but stay at Azumi].[3] But there was the problem of what I'd do if not that, and moreover, there was no one to take my place, so Murakami told me that, given these circumstances, I should think over what was to be done. I'd have been mortified to quit defeated, so I gritted my teeth, tried hard, and got on the right track. I became able to answer the questions they asked me and handle problems that came up.

Just when I was thinking that at this rate I wouldn't be quitting while down, Murakami asked me if I still wanted to change jobs. She said that if I had quit before, when I wanted to quit, the bitterness would have perhaps remained, but now that I myself was satisfied with my job, and since personal relations also had returned to normal, it wouldn't be as if I were quitting in such a bad position, and the bitterness wouldn't remain. So then she asked me if I'd like to change. (Moreover, at this point there were two employees whom Murakami had groomed to replace Usui). For that worst one year, I was totally lost. At first people would forgive me even if I made mistakes, but I wasn't very good at handling the questions some would ask me. So I took responsibility for everything—and didn't have room to move. It wasn't good, but I tried very hard. When I left the group, the person who had subjected me to the most questions, Sakurai, said she understood now how unreasonable she had been in what she had said, now that she knew the job and had experienced it for herself. In the end she said she understood the humanity [*ningensei*] of the *hanchō* and she apologized, weeping. Everyone had said bad things about me, but in the end everyone apologized and said they'd been mistaken. I was very happy. At that point for the first time I was glad I had taken on the job of *hanchō*. I'd suffered with it for a long time, but it was good that I had made such an accomplishment.

It is common in Japanese companies for people to be transferred to divisions of the organization in which they have no expertise, on the principle of sink or swim. I knew one executive who was transferred from sales to the top position in the health and safety division. He had to learn the job from step one, having had no knowledge of health or occupational safety matters.

It is particularly difficult in the beginning when one's subordinates know more about the job than oneself, as in Usui san's case. She commented that the job was psychologically unnerving and that she lost weight because it was so challenging. She had felt that everyone treated her as an enemy at first. It took two years before she felt comfortable in the job and the people understood her well.

It is possible that new supervisors always experience a hazing similar to that of new employees until they show that they have mastered the job and are worthy of it. Although I did not have the opportunity to witness her breaking-in, I did notice some unusual behavior when Murakami *kakarichō* was replaced by Machida *kakarichō* in January 1984. Several people complained that he knew nothing about inspection and was a poor decision-maker, and that the *shisutaa* and some of the other workers were behaving disrespectfully toward him, ordering him about and being lax in their work. It could be that they were simply having a field day after the severity of Murakami *kakarichō,* but they may also have been testing him to see how far he could be pushed.

In any case, Murakami *kakarichō* would not let Usui san step down from being *hanchō* until she had overcome these obstacles and could leave with her head held high. Again we see that at Azumi overcoming hardship is viewed as being for the greater good of the individual who remains steadfast and sees it through to the end.

After leaving I&P, Usui san found herself facing a different challenge. She had been out of production work for six years, and now she had to readjust to it:

> Inspection has a severity about it. Since there were few people, it was easy to achieve discipline, and it was hard to take time off. If one piece came back from the shipping center, it was dealt with rather severely; it was not looked upon lightly. But when I went back to production, on the other hand, I felt the strain of the physical labor. As you don't stop sewing on the machine—it's straight through from 8:30 to 5:00 (with breaks at lunch and 3:00). At first it was hard to get used to, since the environment was so different, but I adjusted fairly quickly because I had done the same work five or six years earlier. Within one month I was keeping up with everyone in the sewing division. I had been used to using my head more as a *hanchō,* but now it was a question of dexterity. My hands couldn't keep up. Plus, the sewing methods of years ago and those now are completely different, so it took a year of hard work to get used to it. Just when I felt it had really sunk in, I returned to the job of handling the outside orders. My present job is also difficult, but not because of physical labor. It's the nervous strain.

Although Usui san said she had not been in her present job long enough, she thought that she might start liking it as she grew accustomed to it. She was not sure if she would stay on until retirement, but she had just taken out a company housing loan that would take ten years to repay, so she wanted to stay at least that long. It is obvious that she was an enthusiastic and talented employee with a determination to keep working. It is also quite unlikely that she would have been able to continue her career at Azumi without the cooperation of her husband and mother-in-law.

## KAMIDA HANCHŌ

Kamida san is if anything even more committed to her job. She, too, joined Azumi at age fifteen and continued through her marriage at twenty and the birth of her two children. As in Usui san's case, her mother-in-law took care of the children while they were young. Kamida *hanchō* is six years older than Usui san, but their experiences within the company were similar. Kamida san, however, has remained as *hanchō,* and was even urged to take the test for promotion in job class to *fukushūnin,* which she passed and which gave her an additional 10,000 yen per month besides her *hanchō* allowance. This meant that, with bonus, she received an extra 300,000 yen per year ($1,250 @ 240 yen to the dollar). No others from her age cohort remain in the shipping center, except for two men.

Kamida *hanchō* came through her early experiences of hazing with her sense of humor intact: she was a vivacious woman, full of self-confidence. Whereas Usui san had misgivings about being *hanchō* and wanted to step down again, Kamida san's confidence seems never to have faltered. Usui san said she had dreamed of being a housewife at marriage, but for Kamida san, work was one condition she insisted on before consenting to marry. When I asked her if she had planned to continue working after marriage, she replied: "Yes, because those were the conditions under which I had my *omiai* [arranged marriage]. "I want to work after marriage. Is that all right?" That was up-front in the conditions. Since they [the prospective groom and his family] said it didn't bother them, I said all right."

In her description of hazing, Kamida said that the trials she underwent hardened her. They certainly left her with a zeal for her work and a passion for a lively and quick-paced workshop. Indeed, one of the difficulties she had in her job as *hanchō* was that of getting the women, particularly the young ones, to work with the same dispatch that she does. She commented:

K: People nowadays are dull [*tsumaranai*]. They're spoiled by the work, you could say. There's no liveliness, is there? Don't you feel everyone is lazy? Whether they're supposed to be in a rush or not, they do it at their own pace. It seems like there aren't any people like me any more, who feel they have to make the deadline if someone says to hurry. In my day, if they said we were in a hurry we had to make it on time. People nowadays don't have that feeling. My group goes at an ordinary pace, so I get fidgety. I get annoyed. At the *chūshutsu han* [selective inspection group] they're pressed for time, so you don't have that. Everyone is frantic.

G: Do you think it's better to be frantic?

K: You're really doing work that way. The reason you are coming to the company is to work, after all. And on the basis of that, you get paid, right? So if you don't keep them hopping, somehow . . . you have to break them in, so you work frantically, and in exchange for that, when there's time you can catch your breath, and you can let things pass. During busy times you have them work hard for you, and in compensation, when you have time to spare, you let it pass even if they're chatting. It's no good to be lazing around day in day out. I've wondered what *you* have thought since you have come, observing that work style. Maybe you thought, "Gee, are they all [lazy] like this?" Don't you think they're a bit sluggish?

G: Well, sometimes . . . but it's hard to strike a balance.

K: Yes, it is, isn't it?

G: If you're too rushed every day, it's awful.

K: But now, downstairs, the new work is terribly piled up. They're doing overtime, you know. Because they aren't putting out during the regular day, they have to do overtime. If that's the case, they *have* to work extra hard during the day. There are times when I can't understand that, since I was brought up in a different age.

I remember my surprise when Kamida san expected me to agree with her that a frantic work pace is better than a steady, ordinary one. In fact, being accused of working at what is called "my pace" is tantamount to being labeled a selfish, disloyal worker (selfish because others are trying their utmost, disloyal because the company has deadlines and needs workers to put forth extra effort at times). To Kamida *hanchō,* activity in itself was valuable—after all, that is the meaning of work, the reason one is paid. In this, she had much in common with the *shitamachi* workers of Kondo's (1990) study. She saw it as a fair exchange; moreover, if she demanded a lot of her workers during busy periods, she would let up a bit when the work load lightened. Workers owed it to the company to adjust to these conditions. If they did not, as was the case with workers downstairs, they ended up having to do overtime—which was more costly to the company and tiring for the workers. What she did not consider was that the shop was often short-handed, and many workers complained that the company was unreasonable in expecting them to do so much in a normal day. To Kamida *hanchō,* the problem was the workers' attitude, not the company's unrealistic demands. She did, however, allow the workers to relax their pace and chat a bit during slow periods. At the I&P, in contrast, the *kakarichō* never relaxed her vigilance.

When Kamida *hanchō* was pregnant, regulations at the company were stricter. The union had not yet negotiated for the extra year of child-care time. Moreover, the work environment made no exceptions for pregnant employees. Nevertheless, Kamida managed to survive the treatment, and, as a result, she now thinks that pregnant women are overindulged and that this is wrong. She commented on the present treatment of pregnant women as a feature of a dissolute age:

> G: You've always been at Azumi, right? Even after marriage.
>
> K: Yes, and had two kids. I did take maternity leave, though.
>
> G: You did? Was it easy? [And what about child-care time?]
>
> K: There wasn't anything like nowadays, where you can go home one hour early [at 4:10]. For my oldest, I worked straight to 5:00 P.M. I asked them if I could leave early but they said that since Grandma was at home, they wouldn't allow it, and they turned me down.[4] With my younger child, I could go home at 4:00 P.M. for just one year. People now get two years, right? It's changed a lot, the treatment. With my older child I didn't go home early and there certainly wasn't any stuff like sitting down if you were pregnant. Even if we were really showing, we didn't sit, we moved around. I think that people nowadays are indulged.
>
> G: Which way is better?
>
> K: Just because someone is pregnant is no reason to treat her respectfully, have her sit, and treat her with care. I think it's best

for a pregnant woman to move around as much as she can. Now-adays, even the people who work with someone who's pregnant will bring her a chair and say, "Please have a seat" and this and that. Even the people around her look upon her indulgently, don't they? If I say, "It didn't used to be that way," I'll just be told, "Well, times have changed," and that's that, isn't it. But I always did it that way—I came through having done it that way. Even when I was pregnant, I was a *shisutaa*. I stepped down once. I was a *shisutaa* until my son was born, and I stepped down when I was really big and I was to begin pregnancy leave. Within a year I was asked to be a *shisutaa* again. Then after a while they asked me to be a *hanchō*, and so I was. I was still young so I could work at a good clip. If it were now, I couldn't do it.

Needless to say, such an attitude on the part of a *hanchō* does not betoken a receptive attitude toward implementing improvements in women's working conditions.

I discuss Kamida san further in the section about family and work, but will add here that she herself said that her work was more impor-tant to her than the household. I wondered if she had a particularly cooperative husband, given her own emphasis on her work life. I asked her which she thought her husband stressed more, home or job. She replied:

> K: My husband seems to do both well, but if it's one or the other, he seems to put more emphasis on work. He doesn't take time off. I guess that I, too, stress work more than home. Grandma always says, "It seems that work is more important to you than the household!" I think this isn't good of me. Somehow or other I always seem to end up giving priority to the company. I think I'd better change my mind about that, but . . . inasmuch as I'm working, it just won't do to change it.
>
> G: You mean there is a conflict?
>
> K: Yes. I think I should change, but I can't. Maybe I'd feel dif-ferently if I were an ordinary (without rank) employee, but since I have responsibility, sometimes I have to sacrifice the home some.

Both Usui san and Kamida san, then, felt responsible toward their work, but Usui, recognizing this, stepped down from her *hanchō* posi-tion and devoted more time to her household, whereas Kamida san always gave her job priority, despite her mother-in-law's criticism and her own ambivalence. From my observation, it seemed impossible to hold a position of responsibility in the company and still run a household; the demands were simply too great.

This finding seems compatible with that of Takie Lebra (1981, 1984, 1992) in her research on career women in entrepreneurial businesses. She found that household support by natal kin—especially mothers—was often instrumental in enabling a daughter to build a successful career. Of the women under present discussion, three lived with mothers-in-law, one with her own mother, and one frequently depended on her husband and sister to manage household and childcare tasks. In cases such as those I present, where household incomes are much lower than those of Lebra's entrepreneurial elite families, the readiness of in-laws to lend a hand in household responsibilities might well increase. Usui san noted that her mother-in-law knew Usui san was suited to work, and that if she intended to continue working anyway, she might as well stay working at Azumi for good, since if she quit once she would never again enjoy the same salary or benefits at any other workplace. So, said Usui san, she gained her mother-in-law's cooperation. It is of no small importance that Usui-san's salary at Azumi was on a par with her husband's salary, and the loss of it would have been a heavy blow to the family finances.

### SHIMIZU SAN

Shimizu san, too, who said she devoted 70 percent of her energy to the company and only 30 percent to her household, had decided to quit the company and give more time to the children's school activities now that her second child was entering first grade. Shimizu san was thirty-one at the time of the interview.

Like Kamida *hanchō,* she lived with her parents-in-law, and like Usui san and Kamida *hanchō,* left the child-rearing up to them. A very resourceful and bright woman, she entered the company at age fifteen. Her family was not well off, and her mother had died when she was ten years old. She said she hardly knew of a world beyond the district where she lived, let alone anything about Azumi, located several miles away in another district altogether. She was quaking in her boots on her first day commuting to the company, worried that she would get the train transfers wrong and get lost. Nevertheless, she soon found her bearings. She became *shisutaa* and then *hanchō* at age twenty-one, and reached the position of *insutorakutaa* (of sewing) by age twenty-four before returning to being a plain employee at the birth of her first child in 1977. She stepped down because she wanted to take the child-care time, and this was impossible for someone in the position of instructor to do:

> There's no way someone with the responsibility of subforeman can take one hour off per day and keep up with the job. Also, one's workers resent it. You don't have to take the child-care time, but I wanted to. Also, you wouldn't be able to ask as much from your workers (if you took it). Usui san was the *hanchō* of the I&P Section, and she didn't step down when she had her first child—she refused to take the child-care time. Yet, after awhile, Usui decided that the job of *hanchō* didn't suit her, so she went back to the sewing division. In my case, I was subforeman over more than one hundred people, not just a *hanchō* over twenty or so. When everyone is working hard you can't just take off early, saying "osaki desu" [I'm leaving ahead of you]. I figured I couldn't handle my home and job well if I kept the post but left early every day. I figured that, whereas you can always get other jobs, you can't do so with your home life. So I decided I'd worked hard for eleven years, and now it was time to take it a little easy for the two years of child-care time, and then work hard again afterward.

In the fall of 1978, Shimizu san's second child was born, whereupon she moved to the Inspection and Packaging division to be in charge of quality control. At this time she also moved her household, from an apartment where she and her husband and child had been living as a nuclear household, to the home of her in-laws. She noted that the only way she could continue working now that she had two children was if they moved in together; otherwise, logistics would become too complicated. Once they moved in, she became responsible only for cleaning up after dinner and doing her own family's laundry every evening. She also supervised her children's homework. The rest, her mother-in-law handled. This arrangement also apparently brightened the life of her mother-in-law, who had become depressed after her son's marriage to Shimizu san but improved greatly after the birth of her grandchildren.

In the spring of 1985, Shimizu san retired from the company, but not with the intention of becoming a full-time housewife. She wanted to find a job as a *paato,* which would allow her more flexibility to attend her children's school activities. In preparation for that, she was using her nine months' unemployment insurance to pay for training as a professional bridal assistant, so that she could find work in wedding halls dressing brides in their ceremonial kimonos. Moreover, she was taking classes in sign language, thinking that that skill, too, might be useful someday. She had also gone to driver's school and obtained her license, increased her activities in her religious organization, and started a high-school equivalency course. She remarked that it was important to stay as active as possible, and that the future looked bright. An added motivation for extradomestic activities was to minimize friction between herself and her mother-in-law. During the interview, which took place before she retired, she commented on this:

> Both my husband and father-in-law feel there's no need for two women to be at home, so they agree to my going out to work and leaving the household affairs to Grandma. They tell me to work hard and save. I think the reason brides and their mothers-in-law don't always get along is they have to see each other twenty-four hours a day. But if one isn't around during the day, the other who stays home can take it easy—stretch her legs—so in that sense, the way Grandma and I are doing it is better for both of us.

With urbanization, women who in the past would have farmed their parents-in-law's land found themselves without employment, except for *naishoku* (in-home piecework). This trend coincided with the rise of the image of the thrifty and industrious professional housewife who remains in the home to serve her family. However, even now that outside work is available to married women, the rationale behind it still remains in the context of working for the household. The modern twist is that this division of labor is seen as a remedy for the age-old conflict between mother-in-law and daughter-in-law.

### NAKADA SAN

Nakada san, who had fourteen years of service at age forty-two, was a widow with one teenage son. Her career offered a sharp contrast to those of the above three women. They had started as fresh recruits from junior high school; she entered the company in midstream. They were go-getters; she was more of a plodder. In her own words:

N: The first place I ever worked was a sewing factory, but not Azumi. I made pajamas and negligees. It was a small company. I worked there for five years. Then, when I got engaged, I quit and stayed home doing nothing for a year, got married, and stayed at home until he died. Then I returned to my parent's house and started working at Azumi in 1970 (at age twenty-nine). At first I was in the sewing division. You'd think I'm healthy just looking at me, but actually I'm not so strong and I couldn't keep up. It was too tiring. So I changed to putting the finishing touches on stuff from subsidiaries and inspecting them.

G: Did you ask to be transferred?

N: Yes, I did. It was within the same section. At the sewing job I felt extremely rushed and couldn't keep up the pace—it was partly line work. In less than a month I was ready to quit. The place I had worked at before wasn't so hard. It was all relatives and friends who worked well together and had a good time. Azumi is a big company and therefore hard, naturally. You enter a point in the line, and if you can't keep up with the flow, it piles up and stops at your station. So I worried a lot and told my mother I wanted to quit, but she said if I said such a thing I could take my child and get out of the house. We had several quarrels over this, with her asking me to leave. Anyway, I changed to the other job, and then, when the I&P Section was set up downstairs, I entered as an inspector and spent about eleven years there.

Here we have a case where the company was willing to find work suitable to the employee. Because Nakada san was able to transfer to a different sort of job, she was able to remain in her mother's household. Her mother's attitude might sound harsh, but in accordance with Japanese society, her own parents' obligations to support her ceased when she married into the Nakada household. Her mother was willing to take her and her child back, but could not afford to support them even if she had wanted to. Nakada san commented on a different occasion that she returned to her own family rather than going to her husband's because she hoped that it might be easier to remarry. However, she never did fulfill this wish.

After several years in the sewing division, Nakada san was transferred to inspecting in I&P and again in 1983 to the shipping center, where she readied cosmetics and leotards for distribution. I asked her why she moved this time.

> Gradually, Murakami began saying it'd be a good idea. I had developed a dislike for inspection work. I didn't want to do that sort of work until I got old. And when defective goods were returned, I had to go to everybody and apologize and I had to stand a long time [on the job every day]. Moreover, Murakami would get angry at me, and once I made a mistake, I'd make another and another. It just so happened that the *kakarichō* at the shipping center asked if there was anyone the factory could spare to work at the shipping center, and Murakami recommended me. I thought any place would be fine if there was a job for me. I'm glad I made the move; I like it better at the shipping center.

Nakada san was obviously not a star worker, but she had managed to stay on for fourteen years. Why was she not pressured to quit? Most workers who were slow at their jobs, made mistakes, or lacked enthusiasm were the first to be pressured into leaving. How did Nakada san manage to stay on? Perhaps it was because management was sympathetic to her household situation, or perhaps it was because Nakada herself never gave the company sufficient reason to try to force her out. In her own estimation she was not a star employee either, but she did do overtime even when she did not want to and was careful to keep her opinions to herself and not cause trouble. I knew her as a quiet person, shy unless you talked to her alone, certainly never offensive to anyone. Fortunately, she was able to settle into a section of the company that she found moderately enjoyable, but she still wished she could remarry and be rescued from having to earn a living. At the end of the interview she confided, half-jokingly:

> If the company heard my interview they'd say they didn't need employees like me, and they'd ask me to quit! I'm only working because I have to. I'm not a go-getter. That's my temperament. I envy people who do things quickly, with dispatch—like Shimizu san, who makes clean-cut decisions. I just mumble and you can't depend on me. Before, when I was at the factory, I wanted to quit as soon as my son graduated, if I had to keep doing inspection. But now that I've changed jobs, I think I can work until retire-

ment. If there were someone who said, "You needn't work, stay at home for me"—someone who would bring in lots of money for me, you know? (laughs).[5]

From these sketches of women workers who have had relatively long careers in the company, one can see some of the difficulties through which one must persevere in order to maintain a job as a regular employee while managing a household at the same time. In Japan it takes a supportive family situation, willingness to go the extra mile for the company, and determination to put one's duty to one's job above one's right to take child-care hours or sick leave, not to mention vacation days. Moreover, it takes great energy and tenacity to insist on staying even when one's bosses or coworkers would prefer one to leave. All these women felt strongly that they owed the company a full day's work. Those who had jobs with some authority were proud that they had made it in a tough system. They had been through the fire. They had learned that, if one is to be effective, one cannot be indulgent, nor can one ask for indulgence. Commitment, devotion, perseverance—these qualities were learned through many years of challenge, and these women could look back on their careers with the feeling that they had earned the respect of their colleagues.

# 6

# *Social Life*

MY COWORKERS often remarked that one of the most important factors in being able to remain at work was the quality of personal relationships in the workplace. I have previously mentioned the emphasis the Japanese place on harmonious group relations and the effort each individual makes to cause as little trouble as possible to her coworkers, giving group interests priority over private concerns. Although concern over the maintaining of harmony in interpersonal relationships is not gender-specific, my informants did feel that the nature of women's interpersonal relations was significantly different from that of men. In fact, it was the general opinion among both women and men that because Azumi was a workplace where women were in the overwhelming majority, personal relations were particularly difficult to manage.

One reason, according to Shimizu san, is that women, unlike men, have no means to disperse their anxieties:

> When there are a lot of women working together, that's the way women are.[1] It brings out the worst in them. I guess women can't just clear away their problems by going for a drink at the end of a tiring day, like men do. Women aren't good at that. They go home angry if there is anything wrong. Men will say, "You want to have a drink?" But women aren't good at saying that. They keep these things inside, where they swell up. They feel like they are the sole heroines in some tragedy and they make a fast exit. It's each per-

son's responsibility to make personal relations around her go smoothly.

Shimizu san does not say that women do not go out drinking because they must attend to household duties. Rather, she says it is because they are not good at that sort of thing and prefer to brood instead. She attributes the problem to a psychological difference between men and women rather than a structural one resulting from differing social responsibilities. Both women and men are constrained to bottle up grievances while in the workplace. *Tsukiai* or what we could loosely translate as after-hours socializing to establish or maintain relationships, allow one to clear the air with coworkers. When drunk, one is forgiven for frank speech; no inebriety, no slack.[2]

Most Japanese I interviewed, both men and women, said that personal relations among women are particularly difficult because women dwell on the past whereas men are less likely to hold grudges. Moreover, they said that women do not take things "straight" but look for hidden meanings, unlike men. Whereas men are *assari*—frank and broadminded—women are overly cautious about detail *(komakai tokoro made ki o tsukau)*, nit-picking. Moreover, men are perceived of as decisive *(warikitte iru)* and unemotional in their work; women, as the opposite: indecisive, emotional *(warikirenai tokoro ga aru; kanjō ga hairu)*. While most interviewees preferred a male supervisor, a few said that only a woman could understand a woman's problems. Some also commented that women's attention to detail is a plus in regards to supervisory work.

Lebra (Rohlen and Steinhoff 1984:43) labels as "routine code switching" the ability to switch from restrained interaction such as that of the workplace to a more informal, intimate mode. She holds code switching partly responsible for the male worker's ability to maintain emotional balance. In assessing the problems of a largely female workplace, Shimizu san indicated that women lack aptitude at code switching, and this has a deleterious effect on their personal relationships at work.

Most women I observed did go straight home after work: when household matters await, there is little time for *tsukiai*. Moreover, when women did participate in *tsukiai*, their behavior differed from that of men. The consumption of alcohol, an indispensable aspect of *tsukiai* among men, is not socially acceptable for housewives and mothers. Women always had the option of having a soft drink, whereas men did not. Some of the women liked their liquor—Murakami *kakarichō,* Shimizu san, and Matsumura *hanchō,* for instance. This may have borne some relation to their status. They did at times go out for *tsukiai* with male coworkers. Moreover, this was particularly true of Murakami san and Matsumura san, who being single and middle-aged, were not restricted by the housewife/mother code of comportment.

It is possible, too, that the higher the status a woman has within the company, the more she is expected to conform to male styles of work behavior. In fact, a woman bureaucrat told me that, as she rose higher and higher in the ranks, the more she was expected to attend *tsukiai,* and the more she was expected to drink. She added that women bureaucrats were also copying other aspects of male business culture, such as playing golf on Sundays. She saw it as regrettable but essential in order to get ahead.

Even on the job, women had different interpersonal relationships from men. One of Azumi's nurses, Takeuchi san, believed that part of the reason for women's generally low status in the company was the way women relate interpersonally on the job. She commented:

> Men are clearly in a vertical society [*tate shakai*]. But women— you get the feeling they're in a horizontal society. With men, from the time they enter there's an order—those above and those below; there is an exact control. But with women, maybe because historically they haven't been working in companies very long, they are not prepared to deal with superiors or to guide those underneath them, as far as I've seen. So if women are to make progress out in society, and it's a vertical society, if they don't do better on that score, they won't make it easily. Women's emotions, you know? They frequently come out. They have to try to get rid of that. They need a more decisive way of thinking. . . . If women themselves don't grow up, I think it'll be very hard for them to develop themselves in the future within the company.

Are women inherently more emotional in their relationships, or does women's low status in the company cause their "emotionality"? Kanter addressed this question in her study of a large U.S. corporation, *Men and Women of the Corporation* (1977:97). She found that secretaries, who had low access to formal means of control within the company, exaggerated their emotionality in order to get what they wanted. Although this strategy often paid off, it also reinforced stereotypes of women as gossip-prone and emotional. Women in Japan, who similarly lack access to power, are similarly likely to use emotional appeals and gossip to gain a measure of control.

The way in which women are organized into groups at work may also affect their way of dealing with each other. Like the bankers in Rohlen (1974), Azumi's men know exactly where they stand in the pecking order and where to set their sights from the time they enter the company.[3] On the other hand, Nurse Takeuchi sees women as "not prepared to deal with superiors or guide those underneath them." How can we explain this?

Company women have little differentiation in status. Women of all ages are thrown together on a daily basis and expected to work harmoniously. The lack of a defined career path and a position to hold within it, coupled with such factors as low rank, lack of time, and cultural space/approval in which to dispel pent-up emotions led women workers to invest their energies and find interests in their personal relationships with each other. These relationships were maintained (and broken!) through countless prework breaks, lunches, and occasional weekend parties or outings.

## *Informal* Tsukiai

As I have mentioned, many women would bring their breakfasts to work. Those who took the early train had time to sit and chat before the day began. Some bought rolls from the canteen downstairs, and others brought their breakfast from home. Hasegawa san usually shared fruit with us, and others also brought food to share from time to time. It was a welcome start to the day, since there was no morning break. This and the lunch and afternoon breaks were the only opportunities to socialize during working hours. Azumi women relied on these opportunities to personalize their surroundings—exchanging food, bringing in beadwork or knitting to work on, retouching their makeup, or polishing their fingernails during breaks, as they made conversation. The only male employee in the I&P, Ishimoto san, would get together with one of the two men from the cutting section during lunch. They would occupy themselves by smoking and chatting at Ishimoto san's desk.

Aside from work breaks, most informal *tsukiai* among women consisted of stopping at a coffee shop on the way home, or perhaps for a light meal if this did not interfere with the schedule at home. Coworkers would also meet occasionally at each other's homes for lunch parties, bringing the children along. Such parties often were held on a Saturday, which Azumi employees had free but employees of other companies did not, so that the women would not inconvenience their husbands. I went to a number of informal parties, where much gossip was exchanged concerning the latest problems at the company, former coworkers' families, or each other's family affairs. Sometimes coworkers took trips together on vacation days. Usually these were older or younger employees who had no responsibility for children.

I use the word *coworker* rather than *friend* because to the Japanese, friendship indicates a long, close, and personal association. A friend is usually a person with whom one grew up and went to school. Although it is possible to form a friendship with a coworker, the supervisors at Azumi actively discouraged this, on the ground that having special friends interfered with the harmonious relations of the workplace as a whole. Rather, one should try to get along equally with all, to separate private from company life.

Apparently, however, this injunction is frequently broken, as I learned during a lunch conversation with Hasegawa san and Koga san during a return trip to Japan in 1988. Foremost in their minds at this time was the difficulty of getting along with other women at work. Hasegawa san remarked that women like to have exclusive relationships with one another. If one friend starts making friends with someone else, the odd one out becomes jealous and begins to spread vicious gossip about her former buddy, forming a new group that "gangs up on" *(yattsukeru)* the former friend, making her miserable by teasing her *(ijimeru)*. The main persecutor usually denies responsibility.

Hasegawa san and Koga san said there is little one can do to remedy this other than to put up with it in silence or confront the perpetrator, as Hasegawa san did. Hasegawa san also recommended withdrawal from any personal contact with the gossiper, talking only when absolutely necessary and only about work-related matters. They remarked that work "friendships" almost inevitably break up in this way, because seeing the same people every day and having to work in groups with them cause interpersonal friction, with many arguments arising over who is or is not pulling her fair share of the work load.

Whereas, they said, men are more frank and open-minded, and are able to shrug off such problems, women's personalities keep them from stable relationships at work.

When I inquired how Hasegawa san and Koga san had managed to stay friends for so many years, they laughed and said they had their fights, but one or the other always apologized and made up, because they could not forget all the good times they had shared. Hasegawa san added that she inevitably makes up because of the *on* (debt of gratitude) she feels toward Koga san, while Koga san said that the pluses still outweigh the minuses, so they cannot help but remain close.

Although there was some fluctuation in the membership in informal group *tsukiai,* members were usually from the same clique or from cliques that got along well with each other. The person organizing the party took great care to invite only those who knew and liked one another. For instance, at the factory there were a number of cliques within the I&P formed loosely around age and/or compatibility. These people ate breakfast and lunch together at separate tables and invited each other to informal parties and other activities on holidays. I was taken in hand by Shimizu's clique, which proved to be difficult on occasion, as Shimizu san did not approve of my socializing with other groups, and particularly with certain members of other cliques. Cliques provided emotional support, but they also created bad feelings among the people of the division as a whole. Tahara san was not a member of Shimizu's clique, and in fact was sometimes the target of the clique's gossip. She realized this, and in her interview with me, noted her disapproval of them, saying:

> I get the feeling that on the surface they act nicely, but I don't know what they're saying behind my back. I hate that sort of thing. I don't think they should say such things in the shadows. I pretty much have an idea who does it, though. When they do such things, things don't go well, do they. You just let them say what they want. Otherwise you get neurotic if you pay attention to every little thing. Therefore, I tell everyone not to let it bother them.

The exclusionary nature of personal groupings among women workers at Azumi differs greatly from the fluid social relations based on "ideological pragmatism" among the male factory workers in Cole's (1971) study. He reported that it was not uncommon for workers who greatly disliked each other to associate after work, and noted that this fluidity in relationships made it easier for the foreign researcher to move among different worker groups with less likelihood of being regarded as a member of any one group. My coworkers certainly were more socially selective, themselves regretfully asserting this to be a characteristic female trait. Although cliques expected loyalty from their members, the boundaries loosened on those occasions when everyone made efforts to act as a larger group. These were the *tsukiai* sponsored by the union or company.

## Formal Tsukiai

There were many formal *tsukiai:* farewell parties and welcome parties, year-end parties and New Year's parties. My coworkers, especially the older ones, often considered attendance at these events to be a burden. They would rather be at home resting. Nakanishi san complained about not wanting to attend the Christmas party, but in the end she bought a ticket and went anyway. She said that the shipping center would lose face vis-à-vis the main office if they did not sell and use their allotment of tickets, so the *buchō* had urged everyone to attend.

The Christmas party was an evening affair, sponsored by the main office, which was held at a fancy hall in the city. It began with a solemn procession of young employees from the main office, dressed as angels, carrying candles to the music of Beethoven. At the crescendo, a large proscenium curtain opened to reveal an impressive backlit stained-glass window. This signaled the official opening of the revelry. The lights came up and the party, an elaborate buffet dinner followed by entertainment by groups from the main office, got under way. Entertainment took the form of well-choreographed and rehearsed jazz dances by leotard-clad young male and female employees. Everyone else was dressed in his/her finest. The atmosphere was gala.

The evening was capped by disco dancing, highlighted by the appearance of the company president. Dressed in casual slacks and a bulky wool sweater, he excused himself for not having had the time to change from his home attire. His dress only served to underscore his charisma, however, and he cut quite a figure on the floor, dancing with several young women at once. They clamored to have their picture taken by his side. Some of my coworkers who did attend later made particular mention of seeing the president out on the dance floor. His glamorous image and the polished presentations of the evening impressed them and gave them pride in working for Azumi.

In contrast, the New Year's party was sponsored by the factory and held at a less splendid hall, on a much smaller scale. The factory manager held sway over the ceremonies; the company president did not make an appearance. Dress, too, was much less formal. The entertainment was provided by the factory employees, with each unit performing a skit or singing songs. The costs were defrayed by the factory, and all employees were strongly urged to attend. The I&P presented a song that we had rehearsed during lunch breaks, all of us dressed in black as members of a choir. Several people from other groups later teased us, commenting that our attire looked more appropriate for a funeral than a New Year's party.

Although innocuous musical numbers like ours were common as entertainment, one group of a few young men presented a bawdy, slapstick skit complete with a broomstick strategically placed to indicate sexual excitement. The audience was in stitches. All told, the factory party was an amateur, homespun affair compared to the glitz and sophistication of the main office Christmas party. The former suggested the cosmopolitan, international image the company is striving to project; the latter, its small-town provincial origins.

There were also outings taken expressly for the purpose of improving group relationships. For instance, shortly after I entered the company, the I&P decided to go on an overnight trip to the company cabin on a nearby lakeshore property. At a special meeting after work we decided when it would be, how much it would cost for food and so on, and who would be responsible for which items. Everyone was urged to attend, but in the end, Ishimoto san (the only man in I&P) and two women who were on the social fringes of I&P excused themselves. These trips were grand social events, with members cooking, cleaning up, drinking, dancing, singing, playing games, bathing, and sleeping together. Women with tots brought them along and they were given free rein on the premises. Indeed, children's enjoyment took precedence over any adult rationale for the evening, as they were allowed to watch TV, volume blaring, while Murakami *kakarichō* made her opening remarks before dinner.

Late at night, after the children had been bedded down, talk would often turn to sex—in fact, one night, at the instigation of Shimizu san, we had a joint question-and-answer session on pre-/and postmarital sexual issues. Typical questions were "How many times have you had sex in one night?" and "Is it true that American men have longer penises than Japanese?" People were particularly curious about my opinions, taken to be typically American. I often found myself at a loss for words. Some of the older women hesitated to participate at the outset, but in the end all joined in. Three of the older women spoke of their distaste for sexual relations with their husbands, saying that they did not respond to their advances, but pretended to sleep, or suffered them passively. Afterward, a few of the older women approached me and asked if I had not been shocked at some of the answers that were given, particularly by the unmarried women, who should not be sexually active. Generally speaking, those under thirty-five seemed to relish such conversations the most. On the whole, these excursions succeeded in drawing the larger group closer together, which was their purpose. For days afterward people would comment on one aspect or another of the enjoyable evening.

## The Morals Keeper

One day I noticed a new sign posted on the wall by the cafeteria stairs: "Let's be careful about how we speak to our superiors and colleagues." When I mentioned the sign to Ishimoto san during our interview, he commented that previously there had been a Morals Keeper, who was responsible for promoting good public manners. For instance, this person would remind everyone to greet one another properly every morning, to say good-bye in the evening, to be sure to let everyone know if one had to step out of the group for a moment, and not to wear street shoes in the workplace. He indicated that he had liked having a Morals Keeper, for it made work relations go more smoothly. As in other Japanese workplaces, at Azumi a great deal of time is spent trying to create harmonious relationships among members of the division, at times including formalized moral exhortations of the sort frequently found in "Confucian" societies and boarding schools.

## Age Differences

In Japanese society, status comes with age. It is commonly noted how the salaryman track aligns work status with age. But at Azumi, where women's work status and age were often independent, it is not surprising that tension in personal relations at work was often intergenerational. There was a wide age range, and those in their twenties or early thirties worked alongside those in their forties and fifties. Many older women employees found it was difficult to get along with the younger generation. Expressing the universal complaints of the middle-aged, they said the young lacked thoughtfulness, were impatient and rude, lacked restraint in their speech, and were selfish and uncooperative.

Tahara san, in particular, had problems with the young, in part because she had been *kakarichō* and was now an unranked worker. Other workers, old and young alike, commented on her pride and temper. When I asked her about personal relations at the factory she replied:

> T: To a certain extent, they are the most vital thing. Age . . . in general, we've become an aging society. Azumi is also an aging society. There are people here who don't quit after marriage, and even after having three kids are coming to work. There are also such people in the sewing section. There really is a great difference in age.
>
> G: Yes.
>
> T: Therefore, it's not very easy—personal relationships. We were born in the beginning of the Showa period. The young generation was born around Showa 35 or 36 [1960, 1961], right? It's like parent and child.
>
> G: Do you think that the way you think about things is different?
>
> T: Yes, it's different. . . . I think it's not a question of agreeing or disagreeing, but of making an effort to get along. . . . Both sides have to try to fit together. I think you know this, but in everything, like in the *kanji* [ideogram] for "person," it won't stand by one stroke alone. The only reason it can stand is that the other stroke is standing too, right? It's just like that. People have to help each other out. When I heard that, it really hit home, especially lately. Even at my age. I wonder if the young people have this insight. It's common knowledge to everyone else.

Whereas most of my coworkers swallowed their anger, Tahara san vented her wrath on more than one occasion. At the shipping center, those who came from the factory had to learn new methods of inspection. This became a problem in my group. Our group leader, who was in her twenties, was poor at teaching but quick to anger if we did not understand her instructions. She usually would fail to provide enough information, and when things did not go as planned, she would blame us for making mistakes. All the members of the group complained among themselves, but no one made her dissatisfaction overt until Tahara san blew up one day, saying, "Are you trying to make a fool of me?" Although, as expected, the group leader did not mend her ways, Tahara san commented to me that she had no other way to relieve her stress.

Seniority in age but not in ability intensified the gap between older and younger employees. This was particularly true when the two age groups did exactly the same work, or when younger people held a higher rank than older ones. In the former case, the younger employees usually had more energy and stamina than the older ones, and sometimes resented having to take up the slack. This was aggravated by the shortage of employees. For instance, one day Nakanishi san told me that she had felt it necessary to warn Tahara san not to be so vocal about her fatigue. According to Nakanishi san's report, earlier in the day a younger employee, overhearing Tahara san complain, asked, "If that's how you feel, why don't you quit?" Tahara shot back, "Just wait until you're twenty years older and see how *you* feel!" Nakanishi san commented to me that if Tahara san didn't learn to keep her feelings more to herself, she would find it hard to continue to work there.

Younger people had to be careful of the language they used when giving directions to older employees. Moreover, the older employee had to learn to defer to the younger without resentment. This is a problem anywhere in Japan where younger employees have authority over older ones. One of my acquaintances, who at the age of forty-eight decided to get a job as a *paato* in a department store, commented that unless older women swallowed their pride and acted like rank beginners, the younger employees would take a dislike to them and refuse to teach them properly, thereby sabotaging their jobs and forcing them out. Even if she knew a better method, my friend was careful not to show it until she was well established within the workplace and had the approval of the younger women.

The young were also criticized for their lack of social responsibility. For instance, when we were discussing what gift to give a group member as her farewell present, two of the young unmarried members of the group ignored the discussion and neglected to contribute to the cost, although the gift was on behalf of all of us. Several older members voiced their disapproval. They felt that they should not have to badger these young women for their contribution, which they should have offered without delay.

Although some perceived the age gap to be a source of trouble, others enjoyed interacting across it. Fujii san remarked that she liked being in a division with so many older women because she could learn so much from them. Nakanishi san liked associating with the younger women, inviting them over to cook with her on holidays.

## Lack of Cooperation within and among Groups

At the factory, where individual targets were the rule, employees were reluctant to cover for their coworkers if they were absent. This was also a source of discontent. Shimizu san explained:

> I'm now working in line work, where each person does one part of the sewing of the total article. There are approximately twenty-six people altogether. But quite a few people lack the group spirit and are only out for themselves. I understand how hard it is on the *hanchō* and sisters because I've been one myself—how hard it is to coordinate the flow of the work. If one person is absent, the others need to take up her slack and cover for her. But some people selfishly feel that they only need to do their own work in such a case, and say we should set the other [absent] person's work aside. I wonder how on earth to make harmony with such people! Especially in line work, even if only one person has that attitude, it won't go well.

Shimizu san is correct in her assessment: Kamida *hanchō* and Usui *hanchō* both gave long accounts of the trouble they had trying to make people cooperate. One would almost think that the greater share of the *hanchō*'s effort goes toward fostering smooth personal relationships.

At the shipping center, where group targets were the rule, the problem was more often one of competition among groups. Groups that achieved less than others on a given day were criticized by other groups. Irahara san said: "My group is doing things of differing colors and styles in small lots, so it takes longer and you can't expect us to keep up with the numbers of pieces other groups inspect. Yet people expect it of us."

The employee's self-identification as a member of a particular group was an obstacle to the smooth functioning of the shipping center's policy of moving employees to whichever group needed extra hands. Not only did employees dislike being reassigned, but there was much bickering over which group needed more help. Doi *kachō* said that groups refused to cooperate with each other, and if there was some work that no group considered its responsibility, it simply did not get done. During morning ceremony we were repeatedly urged to cooperate, an appeal that often fell on deaf ears. Doi *kachō* interpreted this as a problem of breakdown of mutual trust—*sōgo shinrai* —among the workers, which he felt was particularly evident in young people's behavior. He said that they were selfish and spoiled, did not apologize when absent, and caused trouble for others.

## Haves and Have-nots

I did not include a question in my interviews about the sensitive issue of family income. Thus I had no way of knowing the relative financial standing of my coworkers, other than through informal conversation and observation. I could not guess their husbands' income either, since I did not ask for specifics about their workplaces. Most people simply responded that their husbands were *shain* (salaried employees), but salaries vary greatly depending on the company and its size. Nonetheless, competition among the women was obvious. Women who had more money or the goods that money can buy were proud of it and tended to brag about it. Bonus time was the occasion for buying new appliances—microwave oven, washing machine, the latest-model television—or clothing or fancy jewelry. People talked about these purchases as well as their overnight trips to Japanese inns and airplane travel to distant locations.

The consumer was encouraged to narrate. When someone moved to a new house or apartment, as both Hasegawa san and Mihata san did, everyone wanted to know all the details—how big it was, how they had furnished it, and so on. Hasegawa san frequently "complained" that, at the instigation of her daughters, she finally agreed to move to a place that was too expensive and luxurious. She was anxious not to be outdone in being forced into the lap of luxury. After I had visited Mihata san's new condominium, she asked me pointedly if it was larger and more beautiful than hers. Everyone knew that Mihata san was married to a bank employee and both her children were college graduates. It was probably thanks to her modest manner that she was not disliked for this, although I did hear people comment, with a tinge of sarcasm, that she was a wife of quality *(hin no ii okusan)*. Interestingly, in complimenting Hasegawa san on her new place, Shimizu san and others gave most of the credit to Hasegawa san's husband, saying it was because he was so reliable and had such a good job as an instructor at a technical school that they could afford to make the move. This may have helped deflect envy.

According to Doi *kachō,* manifest differences in family financial circumstances caused many problems in personal relationships among the women in the division. He commented that the job status of the husband caused a lot of jealousy and competition among coworkers, and that while most employee's husbands had decent jobs, some were barely making ends meet.

Children's achievements also were the topic of boasting. These included everything from which school one's son attended to which company he had entered. In the case of a daughter's achievements, people were more likely to boast about the good marriages they made than the jobs they landed, but Hasegawa san did speak proudly of her daughter's accomplishments in the computer field.

The size of the bonus each worker received was even a greater source of trouble, as it depended on the individual's performance rather than her family circumstances. Since the amount is tied to evaluations made by supervisors, some who received less felt it was unjust and held it against the supervisor as well as the fortunate ones who had received the superior evaluations. Matsumura *hanchō* complained:

They say, "You don't know my work very well" or "You really know me, don't you!" They say lots of things. Or, even if they think they're doing a good job, sometimes everyone else is doing more than that, or, if one person is trying to do her best, but there is someone else who does even better, then her work just becomes ordinary, doesn't it. There are some people who realize that, but others don't, and it's hard to explain. Some say nothing about it, but I have trouble with others.

Base pay was another sore topic for older workers. The pay scale for F- and G-group workers did not keep rising indefinitely; at some age that management deemed appropriate to the leveling off in ability, the rate of wage increases also leveled off. The employee still got a raise each year, but the percentage was significantly less than she would have received at a younger age. This did nothing to improve the relationships between the younger and older workers, especially in cases where the older employee was actually more productive. Hasegawa san frequently grumbled about this. In the interview she brought it up again:

> Of course, the more [pay] the better. I do want it. But it's out of my control. Because I'm old, you see. It's useless to be at home. And even if I work here for ten years, young people catch up and pass me in salary. If you ask whether I can only do half the work of young ones, that's not the case. Even if I work the same, my pay falls behind theirs. It's very regrettable. But if I went back home there'd be no one to pay me for it! So I've given up. Of course I'd like a lot. Because I, too, work hard, (striving) not to let the young ones beat me. Even if they can't do the work as well as I can, young people get more pay, right? [Perhaps because she only had an elementary-school education.] And the rate at which their pay goes up is greater. I think that's a contradiction. But it's useless [to complain about it].

Frictions arising from differences in age and ideas about appropriate behavior, differences in work pace or style, differences in pay, differences in household income, holdings, and family accomplishments, and problems resulting from identification with one clique or one special friend all make work life challenging. These sorts of problems are ones the company can do little to ameliorate. They are surely part of any workplace that hires individuals of diverse backgrounds and ages, assigns them the same rank, and asks them to work together. Personal relationships can either lengthen or shorten one's tenure of employment. One reason they are so central to women's assessment of job satisfaction at Azumi may be because the jobs themselves are usually not particularly interesting or challenging. The main reason, however, is surely the high value placed on sociability in Japanese culture. Ironically, this very value makes people sensitive to the least disagreement or disparity. As Lebra (1984:56) notes, the more normative emphasis there is on harmony, cooperation, solidarity, and interdependence in a culture, the more likely there is to be conflict. As we have seen, interpersonal relationships at work are a source of both pleasure and stress. Negative self-images, age/work status incongruities, and lack of empowerment all combine to create more divisiveness than solidarity.

# 7

# Improving the Workplace: Channels for Grievances

My coworkers were patient. Considering the pace and tiring nature of the work, they really did not complain much. When they did, it was more often about health problems than about the work per se. Their silence can be partially explained by their ideas about the nature of work. They did not expect work as a regular employee to be easy. Still, every workplace has its problems. If they wanted to voice work-related complaints, to whom did they turn?

Their formal channel for grievances was the union. This, for reasons I shall discuss below, was not a popular choice. An informal channel which sometimes operated effectively was that of the health office. There workers sometimes found a sympathetic ear if not a total solution. They could also organize on their own; not surprisingly, this was the path least often taken.

## Indifferent Bedfellows: Women and the Union

All regular employees at Azumi were obliged to become union members unless they were *kachō* class or higher. Besides management, *paato* were also excluded from Azumi's company union and had not formed a union of their own. As a *paato*, I was not allowed to participate in union meetings, short sessions of five or ten minutes' duration held perhaps once or twice a week during the lunch hour. At my request, I was allowed to attend union events such as the parade on May Day, the summer sports festival, and the monthly after-work get-together where my coworkers decided what to do with the entertainment funds created by their union dues. Until my arrival, *paato* had not been included in the occasional overnight trips afforded by them. When my coworkers voted to allow me to participate in such festivities, they also extended the invitation to the two other *paato* in the workshop.

Unions in Japan are usually enterprise-based. Most of them are also tied to industrial union federations. Whereas the industrial unions negotiate industry-wide conditions such as wage levels and working hours, the affiliated enterprise union negotiates what Koike (1987:315) refers to as "issues that crucially interest rank and file members of labor unions." These, Koike maintains, are promotion, transfer, and redundancy. Wage targets that have been set by the industrial unions during the annual *shuntō* ("Spring Offensive") wage negotiation form the basis for later negotiations between each enterprise union and its firm.

Hanami (1987:40–42) notes three major limitations in the scope of enterprise unions. First, they do not organize nonregular employees (such as *paato* or temporary day laborers). Second, union membership is largely, although not totally, a phenomenon of firms of a thousand employees or more. Third, because most enterprise union leaders are also career-track employees of these firms, they have a strong interest in maintaining a good relationship with management. These considerations limit their bargaining power and tie them more to profitability concerns and to the whims of its corporate leadership than is the case with industry-wide or trade-based unions.

′ This was particularly true of Azumi's union, an affiliate of the textile workers' union *Zensen Dōmei* (The Japanese Federation of Textile, Garment, Chemical, Distribution, and Allied Industrial Workers' Unions), part of the Japanese Confederation of Labor.[1] My informants noted that ever since the establishment of the *sōgo shinrai* (mutual trust) policy, the union failed to secure the level of wage hike obtained by enterprise unions of comparable size within the same industry. By signing the *sōgo shinrai* agreement with the company in 1962, the union declared that they would never go on strike. In exchange for this, the company made a number of commitments. The most important one in practice was the conversion of all workers to monthly salaried employees. Time clocks were dispensed with, and employees were henceforth trusted to observe the company schedule.

They were also permitted to leave the premises during breaks or lunchtime. Moreover, as noted before, if an employee was late to work or had pressing business to attend to, she could, in theory, take up to a half-day off without affecting her paycheck. This provision was separate from the guarantee of paid holidays. The company also promised to accept any written request made by the union. In actuality, my coworkers said, negotiations precede the submission of formal written requests; hence, no requests that encounter serious objections on the part of the company are submitted.

The company president made much of this policy of mutual trust. In my first meeting with him he spoke of it with pride. He boasted that his was a company in which workers and managers cooperated harmoniously. He asserted that never in an American firm would one see such mutual trust, which was possible because he saw the company as a family.

On my first day at the factory the manager echoed the same refrain. After reciting a brief history of the company, he asked me to guess the secret of the company's success. Despite my training in Japanese ethnology, I foolishly replied that I supposed the market was ripe for the company's product just at the time the president decided to sell it: the field was open, and Azumi stepped in. I was wrong; that was not what he had in mind. The reason was spiritual—it was *wa*,[2] the harmony that existed among all the employees, which led the company to greatness. This harmony, he said, extended throughout the organization, and its epitome was the relationship of mutual trust between company and workers.

Since I could not attend union meetings, I decided to include a question in my interview asking the employee how the union was of assistance to her. I had read that in most company unions in Japan, women are underrepresented in the leadership, and that they have little influence over union affairs, ostensibly because the union expects them to quit upon marriage and thus sees no benefit to be gained in fighting for improvements that would benefit women per se (Cook and Hayashi 1980:83–84). However, at Azumi roughly two-thirds of the employees are women and many have long years of service. I thought that perhaps here women would have an active voice in the union.

· I was wrong. For a variety of reasons, women made little use of the union to air their grievances, and the union took little interest in women's working conditions at the company. First of all, the women expected little from the union because they perceived it as weak. Many employees, both female and male, complained about this, facetiously dubbing it a *goyō kumiai*—a union that does the company's bidding. (Despite this, it was a legitimate union, not a bona fide *goyō kumiai*.) Matsumura *hanchō* commented: ". . . Azumi's union is weak. If they had the guts in them to go on strike it'd be great, but they just do what the company says. The union just announces preset opinions, and I get the feeling that even if you offer an opinion, it won't get through. I think it should get much stronger."

Many of my interviewees said that they could not think of any way the union benefited them at all. When I then asked if it would be just as well not to have a union, they conceded that they supposed it helped a bit in increasing wages and bonuses or in keeping employees from being easily dismissed. Ogawa san reported:

O: Everyone is in it. It's compulsory.

G: What good does it do you?

O: No good, to *me* yet, but . . . it's as if we had no union at this company. The company and the union are together at Azumi. It's as if they've signed a pact. When you ask what good it does. . . . Sometimes companies force people to quit. But at Azumi that's rare. It's almost unheard of.

G: Because of the union?

O: If the company tried to force one of us to quit, I think the union would stand up for us. But the company doesn't do that sort of thing, not now. Long ago, the union was the union and the company was the company. But now the union has gone over to the company. They used to ask for larger pay raises, but now they don't. They're neutral.

G: Since when?

O: When there were a lot of Communists. There was a lot of that sort of thing—fifteen or sixteen years ago, I guess. I entered ten years ago. Depending on how you view it, you could say the union has weakened. Nowadays, even union members work hard. And they say that they want pay in return. When the company makes a profit, they want more pay. That's what it's become. In most companies in Japan it's pretty much become that way. So as far as any benefits I get from being in the union, right now there are none for me.

Practically the only means the company has to rid itself of undesirable union employees are the informal ones already described. This could be a sign of union efficacy. However, *paato* are not allowed to join the union, and the two *paato* in my division were dismissed when I&P moved to the shipping center. Most of the workers thought it was a shame, since both of them had long years of service and were diligent workers, but said there was nothing to be done about it.

I wondered what the union's response was to the women's perception of it as a weak organization that had little connection with them other than to collect their dues. I interviewed the secretary of the union, Hayashi san, in July 1985, just before leaving Japan. It was difficult to set up the interview; but it was finally granted and took place in the union's office, inside the main office of the company. Hayashi san was guarded in his speech and rarely answered my questions directly. When I asked him why women employees seemed to lack interest in union affairs, he replied that as times are getting worse for Azumi and wages are not increasing as fast as before, employees complain about what *sōgo shinrai* really means. Hayashi asserted that the union wants to improve conditions. One example of this is that it has pushed the company into accepting sixty as the retirement age for all employees, as opposed to fifty-five, starting in 1985. Yet he did not mention how this policy would affect women employees who, as we have seen, had experienced difficulty in reaching the retirement age of fifty-five. Another union negotiation with the company was to increase the lump-sum payment made on retirement.

Hayashi san criticized the employees for only being interested selectively in issues that pertain directly to them as individuals. He blamed this on the different values of the old and young. I countered by saying that many women I interviewed criticized the union for not listening to their wishes. He replied that it is difficult to communicate with most of the union officials because they only work part-time for the union. They have little time to learn about union affairs, and they do not participate enough. He said that because his directives do not reach the lowest level, they are hard to carry out. Furthermore, he said the reason the union people at the shop level have trouble, aside from time constraints, is that as workers they say one thing and as union members another. They must accommodate two different perspectives, and thereby they lose the trust of the shop workers.

Hayashi san's assessment of the situation has much truth in it. As I mentioned previously in the Kinami case, the person who had to carry out the *kakarichō*'s orders and made Kinami san stand outside the doors of the division was also the union shop representative. And those who, as *shisutaa* or *hanchō,* must be strict about granting vacation days, or who must tell workers to increase the pace, or refuse to allow them to sit if tired, also often happen to be shop representatives. They wear two hats yet must always give priority to the wishes of the company; otherwise the employee might harm her chances of advancement, as Tahara san mentioned, or find herself in trouble with her boss. Usui *hanchō*'s response illuminates this aspect:

> U: It's the company union, right? So . . . I wonder how everyone else is replying to this one . . . I don't think it helps me. It's not quite that they do whatever the company tells them to do, but it's like they are pacifists [*heiwashugi*]. Since they don't think there's anything worth fighting for, it seems that even concerning pay hikes, they end up compromising. I don't have the bravery to bring that up to the union. Perhaps the company distrusts the union, too.
>
> G: Are there those who have the courage to complain?
>
> U: There used to be, but not anymore. People think that it won't do any good to say anything. Since it's a workplace of all women, afterwards you might be bullied by your superiors. Or your superior won't listen to what you say, and so on. Naturally, when you're in a group, if you speak out as an individual, even if what you say is right, others won't see it that way. Because of that, there don't seem to be any people who stand up for their rights. They feel it's useless to speak out—they realize that before they say anything.

The hesitation to air complaints in public is not characteristic of women alone but is a general characteristic of Japanese social behavior. However, women have the additional restraint of being considered unfeminine if they assert themselves. Also, they may be more vulnerable to bullying, as Usui san indicated.

Time constraints are another reason women prefer not to be active in the union. Anyone with a union post must attend extra meetings and study sessions, which take place either in the evening after work or sometimes all day long on weekends. A woman who works at a tiring job that often involves overtime has little leeway in her schedule for union activities. This is mainly because she has family responsibilities as well and rarely is willing to put her family in third place, after company and union. Hence, most women elected to union posts are those who are unmarried or childless. Women with families simply do not want union posts. Thus there are few women in the upper ranks of the union, where what power there is resides. Koga san comments:

K: . . . There's the spring offensive and the bonuses, and the union makes demands such as, "Please give us X amount." As for us, we just listen to what the union says and don't give our opinions . . . because we don't know what's right. So we leave it all up to them.

G: Who decides such things?

K: The bigwigs in the union. The central executive members or the branch managers. There's a branch at the factory and a branch manager.

G: Just one?

K: . . . There's the X branch store. Lots of stores, right? There's one for each store, and these bigwigs, these people in the upper level of the union talk to the company.

G: Are those people women?

K: Almost all of them are men. Women go about as far as being executive committee members underneath the branch managers.

G: Who decides that?

K: I think it's the upper level of the union, as you'd expect.

G: You don't vote on it?

K: That's right. You know, we have workplace delegates. They're the bottom of the union. There's just one representative, a head of the delegates [*shokuba iinchō*]. And we don't want to become one. Because you have to stay after work and come in on Sunday. So it's done by lottery. I've never gotten it. If I did, I couldn't do it.

G: Almost all the people in the union's upper ranks are men?

K: Yes. As far as I know, almost all are.

Thus, although they were members of the labor union, most of my coworkers lacked interest in its activities and considered union duties an unwelcome chore. They also often claimed that they could not understand what went on at union meetings because union officials talked over their heads. The only woman I interviewed who had been active in the union and who had thought extensively about the reasons underlying her fellow workers' reluctance to participate was Ota san. Ota san, as I have mentioned, is, for Azumi, a left-wing radical. How she had managed to keep her job all these years despite her political leanings is something I hope to learn someday. Although she was a shop representative and an executive representative in her early years at Azumi, she has not held office since her children were born. Yet in her spare time she continues to encourage her fellow employees to be more vocal. When I asked her of what use the company union was, she replied:

> O: To an extent, they improved labor conditions, but I think they should understand women's position more. In the union, too, women make up most of the membership but most union executives are men.
>
> G: Why?
>
> O: Mostly it's men who are elected at the union convention. So there are few women activists. So women's opinions don't get heard. Also, in the workplace, women aren't interested in becoming union representatives for the most part. It seems normal to me that if you're a union member, you should become a union official, but it's common for women not to want to be one. It's seldom that women, who after all are working for their own benefit, try to improve their own working conditions. Finally, by now, the number of women who keep working after marriage has increased, but part of the reason for that is that among young people today, the couple can't feed the family on the husband's salary alone. If they rent an apartment, half of his salary is wiped out. Since they can't live like that, they decide they both must work. More than you would think, many people work for economic reasons. But they can't seem to say that their pay is low or that they want more. The union must take that up in negotiations with the company. But I also feel that unless we people at the bottom get more of a worker's consciousness, things won't get much better.

In Ota san's estimation, part of the reason for women's lack of interest is that their social role does not require them to work outside the home. Since they are not socialized to view themselves as workers, they have to be educated to understand that they really are legitimate

"workers" with the right to demand improvements in labor conditions. Intrigued by her answer, I asked how one would raise "worker
consciousness" (her term) among women. She answered:

> It's very difficult. There's a tendency for people to dislike union
> movements. It's social. People think, "What's a *woman* doing
> something like *that* for?" It's gradually lessening, but it's there.
> Rather than spend time on that sort of thing, they think it's better
> to go home and look after the kids. There are more women than
> you'd think with that attitude. So if you want to do something you
> have to talk to each individual to get them to reach that conscious-
> ness—read books, exchange opinions, and so on. But especially
> among the factory workers, there are an awful lot of people who
> can't read. There are also very many who don't like to read the
> newspaper, either. So it's very difficult, given that background, to
> really talk to them. But even so, you can concentrate on one thing
> at a time. For instance, that conflict when your child has a fever
> and you want to go home but can't. You pick up each problem
> from their experience and say, "Wouldn't it be good if the union
> helped with this?" or "The union should be like this," and so on.
> This type of work is very important. But it isn't easy.

I was puzzled by Ota san's comment about some women's inability
to read. According to statistics, Japan has one of the world's highest
literacy rates, 99 percent in 1983 (World Almanac 1985:575). Surely,
I thought, my coworkers were literate, although it was true enough I
rarely saw anyone reading a newspaper or book. Could it be they had
forgotten and lost confidence in reading as the years passed? Many of
them had only junior-high-school levels of education. Although this is
supposedly enough to read a newspaper, it is possible they could have
forgotten some of the more difficult *kanji* (ideograms) over the years.
Those in nonsupervisory positions in the factory had little occasion to
read more than production charts during the course of their work.
Certainly the union handouts were not easy to decipher, with their
elaborate graphs and mathematical formulas as well as texts. The
company's inclusion of *kanji* tests on lower-level promotional exams
also seems to indicate concern with worker literacy. Finally, my colleagues sometimes remarked on my willingness to slog through "difficult" books which had many *kanji* in them as opposed to books that

use more of the *kana* script (alphabetic syllabary), or use *kanji* but add the *kana* along the margin to help the reader with pronunciation. Except for women like Ota san who took an interest in reading, it is possible that many of my coworkers were somewhat under par in literacy. This, in turn, could surely impair their ability to be active at every level of union affairs.

In the interviews I also asked my coworkers what they would like the union to do for them, if it could. The requests were modest and largely directed at the union's own activities, perhaps because of their low expectations of what the union could do for them in dealing with management. Some wished the union would sponsor more activities in which employees could participate with their families. Spouses and children were not invited to the sports festival, for example, and children were not allowed on ski trips and other outings organized by the union, effectively excluding most married women. For male employees or unmarried women, work-related extracurricular activities may not be affected by their domestic situations, but married women cannot make this clear-cut distinction between work and home. Other requests were that the union work to change the company's attitude toward taking paid holidays so that workers could readily take time off, that it arrange meetings to take place during company time and not during the employees' breaks, and that it have the company provide a shuttle bus to transport workers to and from the train station, a ten-minute walk from the shipping center. Only a few mentioned that they would like the union to be more aggressive in negotiating for higher wages and larger bonuses.

In one conversation, Fujii san remarked that she wished the union could negotiate for an on-site day-care center. Actually, several years earlier this request had been made to the company; but, after investigation, the company declared it impossible due to the company's liability in the event of possible physical injury to a child. At that, the union withdrew the proposal and settled instead for one extra year of child-care time.

One of the managers at the shipping center explained to me the company's view of on-site day care. He remarked that it might be worth it to the company as a means to keep women who have special skills, such as experienced seamstresses or designers, but it would be a waste if office women and unskilled workers were to use it, because it would encourage them to stay on the job despite the decline in productivity that comes with age. As the company would not be able to restrict use of a center, it would not be worthwhile to build one.

## Health Section as Advocate

As mentioned previously, I entered Azumi under the auspices of the Health Management Section. During my year at the company, I had some opportunity to chat with the nurses and management staff of the section. The nurses had frequent contact with both factory and office workers, and had firsthand knowledge of their general working conditions as well as their health problems. During individual interviews I held with three of the nurses, they commented that they often found themselves taking on the role of worker's advocate in improving working conditions, a role that one might have expected the union representatives to assume. The reason, they explained, was that at Azumi the union was not very active in nonpecuniary worker welfare benefits. Perhaps, too, workers felt that the health staff would listen to their grievances with a more sympathetic ear, since they were a non-profit-making section specifically established to promote worker health and were professionally trained in occupational health management. Finally, the somatization of stress is culturally acceptable, whereas bringing a problem into the open is not. If they could not ask the *hanchō* for indulgence, at least they could be assured of some TLC at the Health Management Section.

Yet it was not easy for the Health Section to bring an individual's problems to the company, since there was no set procedure or system to follow. All the nurses I interviewed commented on the powerlessness of their position for negotiating with the company over improvement of working conditions or settling the work-related health problems of specific individuals. Takeuchi san explained:

> Although Japan has a Safety Law covering companies, it's weak in terms of authority. [The law is not enforced by an outside agency] but is left up to the company to carry out. There are no legal [implementing] regulations, not even one requiring a company to hire nurses. The company will put nurses in only if they really think health care is important. Also, health management itself is

entrusted to the managers of the company and their philosophy, so it's very insecure. Moreover, amid the pursuit of profits, it's difficult to make good PR for the Health Section and show how much use we are, because we don't make them a cent.

Miyazawa san gave more specific examples relating to this problem:

> The Health Section has no power because it makes no money. When the fortunes of the company go down, so do the fortunes of the department—the company won't carry out our requests. When finances are good, work is easy. When the company gets into rough times, though, each employee pushes him/herself too hard. Even sick people who know they shouldn't be overdoing it put in overtime or go out on business, and I can't tell them not to. When sales go down, I can't lend employees a helping hand anymore. It's a pity. I wish the personnel department had as much weight as the sales department.

Yamada san likewise complained: "I want to take good care of the patient, but I can't do this well in a health-care department that's under the thumb of the personnel department. I have to do what the company says."

I asked the nurses if there were any issues they would like to see the union address. Takeuchi san had three suggestions for the union: (1) Get the employees an exercise room; (2) Make it easy to take personal holidays; (3) Make the company stop pressuring women to quit when they marry or have children. Ultimately, she wanted the union to change its thrust: "As [the company] stabilizes, I want a union that understands that it shouldn't just concentrate on getting more money [that is, salary increases], but also should try to make it a place where women can feel peace of mind working, a place where they can have equal opportunity."

Miyazawa san's suggestions were slightly different. She wanted the union to fight the company to improve pregnancy and birth protection. For instance, she would like Azumi to institute a policy of flextime for pregnant women during rush hours, as many other companies do. Moreover, women who worked in the factory could not take snack breaks when they were pregnant, as could the office workers, so it was especially difficult for them to get through the morning hours, which have no break. She thought the union should take care of this problem. She also wanted them to increase women's salaries. Her particular concern about salaries may in part be related to the fact that she had recently lost her husband and was now finding it difficult to get by on her salary alone. She explained earlier in the interview that previously her income was supplementary, used for "extras" and for leisure activities, but now it went entirely into daily necessities; and even so, it was a tight squeeze. She also thought that the pay allowances for *shisutaa* and *hanchō* were awfully low:

> It's ridiculous at 2,000 yen ($8.33 at 240 yen/$1) or 4,000 yen [a month]. The union should negotiate that. Women have to push too, but really it's the union that should make the effort. But they say that even if you say such things to the union they won't bring them up for you, despite the number of women here. Perhaps it's because they [the women] are not bothered enough by it. Individually they complain, but. . . .

I asked her if she means that the women have to get together more. She replied: "Yes. The things that they actually should be bringing to the union, they complain about to me [and the other nurses] instead."

On a return trip in 1988, I learned that the company had removed the Health Section from the company grounds altogether. These nurses and the psychologist were working at the Labor Health Insurance Office, where employees could go for a consultation if they wanted one. The manager who related this news said it was a blow to health care at Azumi. Workers had to go out of their way for an appointment, so many would probably go untreated. He echoed the nurses in noting that the Health Section had never had much power in decision-making, as it was not a revenue center.

It was obvious from their conversations that my coworkers were very anxious about working conditions. Yet they never expressed a desire to have the union improve those conditions. I asked Hayashi san what the union would do to improve women's conditions so that they could work until the new retirement age. His response focused on wages. He said the wage curve must be changed, but that one cannot improve conditions such as lack of a morning break or the difficulty of taking holidays without changing (i.e., lowering) wages. I then asked if he could not ask the company to give women more varied work so that they could stay on until retirement. He responded that they cannot personalize their regulations; if they did, then those who did not benefit would dislike it.

When I asked him to be more specific, he gave the example of *ikuji jikan* (child-care time). By law, child-care time is allowed for one year. At Azumi, thanks to the union's negotiations, the period was extended to two years. Formerly, the employee's bonus was the same whether or not she took the time. However, the company was dissatisfied with this state of affairs because the production rates of those who took the leave were lower than the rates of those who did not. So the union negotiated for two extra weeks' maternity leave in exchange for a 3–5 percent cut in bonus for those who take the child-care time. The union thought the women would want the extra two weeks more than the money, but those who felt that way were actually in the minority. Most women wanted both the two weeks' extension and the full bonus money! I asked Hayashi san what would happen if the employee refused to take the extra two weeks, and the reply was that her bonus would still be cut as long as she took the child-care time.

I failed to ask him what would happen in the case where an employee took the extra two weeks but forfeited her child-care time. There are precedents for this. In the past, some women, with their doctor's permission, have taken maternity leave beyond the twelve weeks required by law. The company's loss in such cases is that it is inconvenienced in production, but it is the labor union's health insurance that pays the employee's wages during maternity leave. The insurance pays 60 percent of the worker's wages for the duration of the twelve-week leave; the company does not make up the difference. I do not know if the health insurance continues to pay the worker's wages during this extra two-week extension. If it does not, and if, as likely, the company does not step in to cover the employee, then it is no wonder that no one thanked the union for its efforts—it had negotiated away 3 to 5 percent of their bonus in exchange for a two-week extension in maternity leave which the worker probably could have received anyway.[3] With more and more women taking maternity leave and child-care time in the past few years, the company undoubtedly realized that it would come out ahead in this "exchange" of maternity extension for bonus cuts.

Hayashi san expressed indignation that the union had fought so hard to help women gain this extension only to find it was not appreciated. He commented that the union had thought the most important thing was the women's health, and that it was doing them a favor by getting them two extra weeks of rest. He noted that old customs do not fit the present age and the company wants to change them (he was again unspecific). He acknowledged that some employees felt that the new policy represented a worsening of the labor conditions. Other "customs" that the company felt were outdated were probably those of restricting overtime and nightwork for women and the nominal provision of menstrual leave. These provisions in the Labor Standards Law were under fire by industry representatives, who wanted them to be abolished with the enactment of the Equal Employment Opportunity Act.

I also asked him what changes Azumi would make in order to conform to the Equal Employment Opportunity Act. He answered that Azumi already conformed to 90 percent of its provisions and added that there are no company regulations that need to be changed. I expressed surprise and asked him about promotion policy. He said that some want opportunities for promotion and some do not, so you cannot make a blanket rule about it. Both men and women have a chance at promotion. One thing to realize is that people are employed according to the type of work *(shokushu)*. You make an employment contract when you enter the company, and that contract stipulates the job and what it entails. It is not that there is no promotion track, just not in those job categories. He did not explain why so few women are in the job categories that have these promotional tracks.

Hayashi san's last comment was that many women do not want to work at Azumi until the retirement age of sixty. Time and again my coworkers had expressed their worries about whether they could actually make it to retirement. The fact is, however, that they failed to communicate this effectively and forcefully enough for the union to heed. This is apparently a common situation, and Azumi's union was probably about equal to others in its handling of women workers' concerns per se. Here a comment of Diane Simpson, from her study of Japanese unions and women workers, is helpful:

> Sex discrimination has been so institutionalized that most are only marginally aware of it. Disgruntled women tend to keep their workplace grievances to themselves and try to adapt, making it unlikely that unions will actively seek to eliminate discrimination against women in the near future. . . . For major changes to occur, there will

have to be a push from women themselves, but the current situation does not make that likely, since most women are not very critical of their work situations. (1985:224)

Simpson did not see much militancy and organization on the part of women in unions, nor did I at Azumi. As she says, women are for the most part uncritical of their situations, or, if they are critical, they do not seek a formal audience in which to address these problems. Rather, they put up with conditions as they are and focus their remaining energies on their homes and families.

## Self-Advocacy, Self-Interest, and Amae

When I asked why Azumi did not routinely give women employees more varied work so that they could stay on until retirement, Hayashi san couched his reply in terms of exceptions and fairness. At the time his answer struck me as being obtuse, deliberately skirting the real issue. Actually, his answer reflected a philosophy shared by many of my coworkers, applied to other situations.

In Japan, being perceived as different from others is more often a minus than a plus. Members of a group should act alike, and self-interest should take a back seat to group interests. At Azumi no exceptions were made, even for those whose handicaps prevented them from keeping pace with those around them. Recall Taniguchi san's account of having to adjust to the pace of those around her. Some coworkers complained that she was *amaete iru,* asking for indulgence, when she wanted to work sitting down and have her targets adjusted downward. They would not or could not recognize that she was doing her best. Nakanishi san made similar comments about a legally blind young woman at the shipping center: she said that she was being spoiled, and it was about time that she be given more rigorous targets.

My coworkers clearly felt that the workplace is not an appropriate arena in which to seek indulgence. That is for the realm of the hearth, and the most successful women at Azumi noted time and again the need to keep the two strictly separate. We have seen that Murakami *kakarichō,* who saw giving up as self-indulgence, urged my coworkers to win out over adversity rather than seek an easy way out. Kamida *hanchō,* too, wanted 100 percent effort from her women, whether they were young or old, pregnant or not. As long as they were workers in her group, she expected the same from each of them. Anything less would mean they were asking for indulgence. An employee who asks for medical leave for shoulder, neck, and arm syndrome (carpal tunnel syndrome) opens herself up to being labeled as an indulgence-seeker. Asking for special dispensation is considered selfish and unfair, no matter what the circumstances.

Even so, Nakanishi san complained very much about the implementation of a new system of testing employees to determine precisely the average time required to do a given task and to make that the standard for everyone. Of course, only about half can be above average, so this would require the other half to work faster. She said it was part of the company's tactics to rationalize production so that fewer employees could do even more work. Those who could not meet the standard would have a hard time and would probably end up having to quit. She thought this would pit older workers against younger and make personal relations even more difficult. She seemed less sympathetic to differences resulting from handicaps than to those resulting from age.

In a different situation, but with similar reasoning, Koga san and others complained to me that because the fees for their day-care centers were on a sliding scale, they ended up paying more than women whose income was lower. The children were the same; it was unjust for them to pay more.

When standards are relaxed to take into account individual circumstances, it is seen as inequitable. This perception divides younger employees from older, unmarried from married, the childless from those with children, the healthy from the well, and is a formidable barrier to group efforts to improve working conditions.

For instance, one day in the second year of my research, I went for a visit to Hasegawa san's house. She and Fujii san were there, talking about what they thought was the latest tactic of the company to force women with children to quit: a plan to change the operating hours of the shipping center to conform more closely to those of the department stores. This would mean that the workday would start and end half an hour later. Thus they would not be out the door until about 6 P.M. if the proposal were implemented. Fujii san was upset because she had two children in a day-care center that closed at 6 P.M., making it almost impossible for her to get there in time to pick them up.

The company was taking a poll, asking who absolutely could not manage if the hours were changed. Fujii san said that the majority of the married women were unhappy with the change. It meant they would have to shop even later for the evening meal, a special hardship in the winter when shops close early. Dinner preparation would be delayed a half-hour, and it would make days with overtime especially difficult. Nevertheless, they said they could manage somehow. Moreover, the younger workers without family responsibilities had no serious objections. There were only five women who said they would be severely inconvenienced by the new hours, all of them mothers who had young children in day care.

Fujii san wanted to know my opinion. I told her I thought that she should point out to the other women the mutual advantages to be gained by forming a united front on this issue—after all, the unmarried workers or the ones without children might one day find themselves in a similar position to hers, if they continued to work. And the older women with families would be glad not to have the inconvenience of arriving home that much later each day. Fujii san told me that it was very difficult to get people to agree on such matters; each was too worried about the security of her own job to go out of her way for someone else's benefit. People just didn't think that way, she said, and moreover, the union was weak and would not listen. She was determined to stick with her job no matter what, so she did not want to risk her neck by stirring up things with the union. Fujii san said she would not let this defeat her; even if the hours did change, she would find a way to continue working. As it turned out, the company decided not to change the hours—at least for the time being. Later the company did indeed change the hours, but Fujii san was able to make arrangements to pick up her children as soon as work let out.

Anne Imamura (1987:109–110) encountered similar viewpoints in her research on urban Japanese housewives and participation in community action groups. According to Imamura, women look to the government to solve their problems, because, for a variety of reasons, they are not able to organize and push through desired reforms on their own. She recounts the case of a woman who tried to keep a highrise building from being constructed next door:

> . . . She lives in a condominium, and when the new building was proposed, her condominium had a residents' meeting. At first everyone was willing to sign a petition against the new building, but when it was discovered that only her side of the condominium

would be affected, others refused to sign. . . . Although other residents had been asked to do no more than sign a petition, they were unwilling to do even that because the problem was not theirs.

Forming a united front behind an issue that does not immediately or directly affect all equally, then, appears to be a difficult if not impossible task. In this case, the "community" in question was that of dwellers in the same condominium. Imamura found that the women who lived in this community lacked a well-developed sense of neighborliness or mutual interdependence. Their energies were focused almost entirely on their individual families, and rarely did homemakers spend much time on activities that did not concern their families' well-being.

One might think that the sense of community among women at Azumi would be strong enough to garner support for measures to improve women's working conditions, but actually this was not the case. As Fujii san observed, women at Azumi were too worried about their individual jobs to risk organizing behind this issue. It would have been very difficult to convince those who were not affected by the change to lend their support. Those who asked that the hours not be changed were easy targets for accusations of being indulgence-seekers.

There is yet another dimension to the question of women's lack of solidarity. As we noted in Chapter 1, in choosing to work despite being married with children, Azumi's women workers were challenging the widely held gender role model that places women in charge of the household. Many of my coworkers were in households where, by working outside the home, they were treading on thin ice. If they were to unite and confront the company over some issue, this would strain the situation further, because housewives and mothers are not supposed to show such serious intent with regard to their jobs. Such action would be yet another indication that work was gaining priority for them over the home.

If Imamura's housewives were reluctant to participate in time- and resource-consuming extradomestic activities, how much greater are the constraints on mothers who work full-time. We shall now turn to the domestic arena, exploring how my coworkers fulfilled their roles as wives and mothers.

# 8

# *Budgeting and Day Care*

IN THE 1980s Japanese "office ladies" gained the reputation of being consumers par excellence. From designer clothes to European holidays and shopping junkets wherever the high yen would lead them, these young, unattached women are characterized by high spending and a carefree attitude toward work. My blue-collar coworkers offered quite a contrast to this consumer jet set. How much did they make, and on what did they spend it?

Although my coworkers did not hesitate to ask me my income and that of my husband, many were reluctant and embarrassed to discuss their own financial circumstances, even when I approached the subject in an indirect way. As Doi *kachō* remarked, women coworkers were sensitive about the relative disparities in their household incomes. They may not have wanted to reveal this information to a foreigner in their midst who would be interacting with them for an entire year. In any case, I decided against asking about household income, but I did ask how each spent her income.

I learned that most married women spent their incomes on housing, education, and daily living expenses. Those with small children often spent much of their income on day care. Nishitani san volunteered information on her salary: 1,500,000 yen per year without bonus and after taxes, or approximately 2,000,000 yen per year including bonus and taxes. In 1984 the exchange rate was 240 yen to the dollar, yielding a salary of $8,333. Her salary in 1993 exchange rates would be over twice this. Nishitani san is a high-school graduate with sixteen years of service. When I asked her how she spent her income, she replied:

> Hmmm . . . child care. I pay 65,000 yen for my two children, and rent is 60,000 yen. With that my salary is completely gone. Also, insurance for the children and my husband. Since the children are little, my husband's insurance is more. Other than that, there are living expenses, food, etc. So with rent and child care my salary is all gone. And with pocket money for Father (my husband) and insurance and liquor money, that takes half his salary. The rest we put toward food. We just make it.

Ogawa san, who had a mortgage to pay and educational expenses for her son, responded:

> O: We're paying off our loan. And the younger child likes baseball, so he's going to a high school in Shimane prefecture where baseball is their specialty. He's in a dorm—for three years. This year he'll graduate. It's lonely without him. That costs a bit of money, so . . ."
> G: I see. For his education.
> O: Yes. With that, we hardly have any savings.

Mihata san was a *paato* whose children had grown. Her husband worked for a bank, and they put both children through college. They were living in a new condominium. She replied: "Until now, when the kids were going to school, although I received my salary, it went for living expenses before I knew it. Now my children are working and don't need money. So I buy things for myself and save the rest for the household. And my daughter has a baby. I buy the baby things. That's about it."

From my interviews I received a strong impression that women with children at home spent most of their incomes on educational and living expenses, perhaps saving a bit if they could, and occasionally making a purchase of clothing or some other personal item that they would consider too extravagant or frivolous to buy with their husband's income. As children grow and leave the household, women's incomes become freed to a certain extent from the pressures of daily living expenses, so long as their husbands remain employed. Ota san, whose children are teenage, lives with her in-laws rent-free. Her husband's salary covers all their living expenses, so she uses her own toward leisure activities and savings.

Even after children mature, demands on their mother's income may still remain. For instance, Hasegawa san's twenty-nine-year-old daughter married in 1989, to the great relief of her mother, who had worried about having to support her after she and her husband retired. This daughter married three years later than the average age because she had no outside job, but spent her time taking care of the house and preparing meals while her parents worked full-time. Her natural shyness was compounded by the lack of opportunity to meet potential spouses. Hasegawa san spent a good deal of her income on matchmaker fees, and then on her daughter's dowry, wedding ceremony, and honeymoon, to assure that she would marry and be well provided for in the future.

She also spent much money on gifts to her younger daughter's baby. This daughter had married two years before, and Hasegawa san said she felt she had to give an elaborate *omiya-mairi* (first shrine visit) outfit costing 250,000 yen (about $1,040 at 240 yen/$1) and other gifts to the baby in order for the daughter to be well respected by her in-laws. One might surmise that the daughter had married an eldest son who coresided with his parents, but this was not the case. Hasegawa san was extremely sensitive to protocol and wanted to assure her daughters' smooth transitions into their new households.

Not every woman feels such a long-term financial responsibility for her children. Fujii san, who came from a poor urban family, told Hasegawa san and me that it is enough to raise the children until they are finished with schooling. After that, they are on their own. She said her own parents could not afford to give their children much besides the basics, but that was enough, and she did not feel she had suffered from this. Hasegawa san was much more concerned about others' opinions of what one should do. Her age may have been a factor; at fifty-two, she was a generation above Fujii san. Her background could also have been influential. She was a farmer's daughter who migrated to the city after marriage.

Nakada san, widowed and living in her mother's house, still depended on her mother to keep the household accounts. She answered: "I pay for food and the rest I use for pocket money for myself and my son—I buy things for him. I don't save. I don't have enough to. I leave social security and so on up to my mother. I don't bother with banking. Mom does it all."

Those who were unmarried and living at home[1] spent a greater amount of their incomes on clothing and leisure. Most of them also contributed some money to their parents' household expenses and saved some for their future marriages. Murata san commented: "I use it on fun, clothes, pocket money. I put some into the household."

Taniguchi san, still living with her parents at the age of forty-seven, replied:

> T: I'm free to use it as I please. To some extent I save. I use it on clothes and food, that sort of thing. I do save about 30 percent of my income.
>
> G: That's a lot.
>
> T: I don't think so. If the family's in trouble I give my parents money when I get my bonus and every month I hand over an amount to my parents.

Murakami *kakarichō,* who lived in the rented house where she grew up and whose parents are deceased, said:

> First, living expenses. After that I have no special plan. I spend what I get without reserve. My living expenses are food and drink. After that I buy what I please. Rent is cheap, not even 10,000 yen ($41 at 240 yen per $1) because I live in the [rent-controlled] house where my father grew up. I spend what I get without thinking about it. It's not thirty, forty, or fifty thousand yen like some people's rent is these days.

Murakami san also mentioned that she was saving money in order to open a small restaurant when she left the company.

Travel abroad was very unusual for Azumi factory women. Just before I left Azumi in August of 1984, one young woman married and went to Europe for a honeymoon. It caused much excitement. Most travel was domestic—to the beach in the summertime, to one's family's hometown at New Year's, to a hot springs or perhaps a town known for its pottery, if there was the time and means. A few people dreamed about taking one trip abroad after they retired. Trips abroad were certainly not taken for granted.

Along the same line, the clothes my coworkers wore, while certainly very nice and of high quality, were not designer fashions, and people were more likely to boast of the bargains they had found than the names they had bought. Employees took advantage of special in-house sales to stock up on Azumi lingerie and other apparel that would be beyond their reach at normal prices.

## Managing the Purse

When scholars argue that Japanese housewives' social status is high, they often point to their autonomy in household decision-making and firm control of their husbands' salaries (Ueno 1987a; Vogel 1978). In her study of urban Japanese housewives, however, Imamura (1987:81) found women's hold on the purse to be somewhat weaker than the literature indicates:

> The income data I received were often vague, but generally a certain sum is set aside each month for the wife to manage. Wives know their husband's salary, but they do not know whether he received any other payments . . . or simply do not pay attention to such payments. The wives I interviewed pointed out that a great deal of the monthly salary never reaches home anyway. The company deposits it in the bank, which automatically deducts utility, housing, and credit payments each month. From whatever is left the wife has to manage food and clothing and in some cases put money aside for children's schooling.

I found some variation in the grips in which my coworkers held the household purse. While some managed finances entirely by themselves, others indicated that their hold was light and their husbands had free access to money. Those who lived with in-laws either gave their salaries and those of their husband to their mother-in-law to manage or worked out an arrangement whereby the grandmother kept general household accounts and the daughter-in-law managed some of her family's funds separately.

It would be difficult to find a way to measure accurately who has "control of the purse" and to assess the impact this has on relative power of household members. One thing is certain: no one told me her husband took charge of the finances.

## Day Care

If a woman is to stay on at her job throughout marriage and childbearing, access to dependable and low-cost day care is essential. Most of my married coworkers had two children; some had three. Who looked after them once maternity leave was up?

Taking into consideration the ideal type of the "education mama" who devotes herself full-time to domestic nurturing, one might expect to find a dearth of public day-care institutions. Yet that is not the case at all. In 1982, there were 22,714 licensed centers—59.75 percent public and 40.25 percent private—caring for 1,958,720 children (*Hoiku Hakusho* 1983:300–301). The number of centers and registrants has remained fairly constant in recent years, with a slight decline, reflecting the shrinking of the number of births. In 1986 the total number of licensed centers was 22,879, with 1,808,000 children enrolled (Sōmuchō Tōkei Kyoku 1988). Besides licensed centers, there are also *hoiku mama san,* "day-care mama," *katei hoiku seido,* "home day-care system," *hiruma sato oya* (day foster parent), and round-the-clock operations called "baby hotels."[2]

Osaka established the first public center in 1919, as an urban relief project *(saimin kyūsai jigyō).* Kyoto and Tokyo followed in 1920 and 1921. The number of public centers grew with unemployment and poverty in the first years of Showa (from 1925). They saw another marked increase after Japan went to war with China in 1937, as more women entered the non-home work force (Hashimoto 1982:139). The number of public day-care centers increased from 879 in 1935 to 2,184 in 1944. Still, Hashimoto points out that the national government regarded day-care centers strictly as measures to aid the poor, certainly not to support women's liberation into the work force, as in the Soviet model. Plans for their organization and maintenance were left up to the prefectural and local governments. They received supplementary funds from the national government under the Social Enterprise Law *(Shakai Jigyō Hō).*

With the enactment of the Child Welfare Law under the occupation government in 1947, day-care centers were given a solid mandate by the government. Whereas the Social Enterprise Law of 1938 only provided for subsidies or supplemental funds, now the centers were guaranteed full funding by the municipalities and the state. Ironically, most

Japanese women with whom I have spoken on the topic assume that American women are at least as well if not better provided for vis-à-vis government sponsorship of day care, maternity benefits for working women, and so on, since it was during the American occupation that Japanese laws were put in place to provide such benefits.

The postwar baby boom and nationwide poverty conditions strengthened the demand for day care. The number of centers steadily increased. The government decided to bring private centers established in the prewar period into the fold, subsidizing them along with the new public centers and subjecting them to the same operating regulations as public centers (*Hoikuen 110 Ban* 1984).

As there were too few centers for the number of applicants, municipalities put conditions on admission. For instance, the City of Osaka gave preference to the poor, families with working mothers, families where mothers were ill or pregnant, families with many children, and motherless families. Centers still have conditions for admission. In Tokyo's centers in 1983, applicants had to fall into one of the following categories (*Hoikuen 110 Ban* 1984:26–27):

1. Mothers who work outside the home and therefore cannot take care of their children.
2. Mothers who do *naishoku.*
3. Households where mother is not present (missing, in prison, etc.).
4. Mothers who are unable to care for their children due to childbirth, illness, or physical or mental handicap.
5. Mothers who are nursing the sick or handicapped at home over a long period of time.
6. Households that have suffered disasters (fire, flood, earthquake).
7. Special cases, for instance, full-time students or those in training to return to work.

Whereas Taisho era regulations considered the family as the unit to be addressed, it is apparent that current regulations assume that mothers are the ones responsible for their children's upbringing.

Up until the 1960s the majority of center users came from poor families who paid few or no taxes. This changed gradually as Japan became more prosperous. Whereas 17.26 percent of registrants came from the top income tax category in 1961, 53.31 percent came from this category in 1976 (Hashimoto 1982:144). Licensed centers continue to give priority in admissions to full-time working mothers and low-income households, but there are fewer of them now.

Both public and private centers receive government funding and operate on a sliding-scale fee basis. Nevertheless, tuitions rose dramatically from the late sixties through the seventies, from 6,600 yen as the top rate for a child under age three in 1967 to 47,000 yen in 1977 (Hashimoto 1982:169). (Fees for older children are less, and fees for the second child are half those of the first.) In 1988, the top rate for a child under three in Tokyo's wards, which are the least expensive in the nation, was 48,000 yen (*Paasonaru* Jan. 1, 1988:45). Hashimoto attributes the increase in fees on the one hand to improvements in the conditions and training of caregivers and, on the other, to a reluctance on the part of the government to absorb these costs. In her estimation, the government keeps day-care costs high for the average dual-income family to encourage women who lack special skills or talents to quit at childbirth and return as *paato* when their children have grown. In her example, the 1976 average income for a woman worker was 82,000 yen per month in companies of over ten workers, or approximately 1,500,000 per year including bonus. This means that with her and her husband's combined incomes, they would probably have to pay the top rate at a day-care center for their child under three, or 47,000 yen a month. She argues that such high costs lead women to quit work (Hashimoto 1982:169).

Japan also has a system called *gakudōhoiku*, whereby children who have no one at home at the end of the school day can remain after school in a day-care program on the grounds. There were 4,739 such programs nationwide in 1982. By and large, these are concentrated in the cities: 64 percent of municipalities, 100 percent of "special" wards, 8.2 percent of towns, and 2.7 percent of villages have *gakudōhoiku* (*Hoikuhakusho* 1983:119). At Azumi, Fujii san moved her family to a school district that had *gakudōhoiku* when her daughter entered first grade and needed after-school care.

Day-care issues of concern to working parents in the 1970s and 1980s have been spiraling fees, the lack of availability outside the normal 8 A.M. to 5 P.M. day, and the reluctance of centers to provide care for infants. Although at first glance it may seem that Japanese women workers are blessed with bountiful day-care facilities, my coworkers pointed out that it is not easy to find a center which will accept an infant, and day-care center hours may be inconvenient. Hashimoto points out that, in December 1977, the number of infants less than one year old in day-care centers was 25,659, only 1.6 percent of all children in day care.[3] She further states that the government is strongly opposed to increasing public day care for infants. The Ministry of Welfare, citing harm to children, has also objected to lengthening day-care center hours (Hashimoto 1982:166). Nevertheless, in 1982 it issued a notification to day-care centers indicating that an extension in normal hours of operation to approximately 6 P.M. would be in order. By 1988, a 6 P.M. closing had become the general rule for city nurseries, with some extending to 6:30 P.M. or even 7:00 P.M. to allow for long commuting time.[4] Nationwide, however, only 50 percent of centers are open past 5 P.M.

Some workplaces supply day-care centers for their employees, but they are by no means common. Hashimoto counts a total of forty day-care centers in industry (All Electrical Workers, twenty-six; All Communications Workers, ten; All Printers, four). By 1978 all public universities had day-care centers, beginning with Hokkaido University in 1958. They are also common in hospitals, where there were four hundred centers in 1978. She notes that corporate-based day-care centers suffered cuts after the oil shocks in 1973–1974.

In the spring of 1985 I sent a questionnaire to those Azumi factory women who had children of junior-high-school age or younger, asking about their child-care strategies. Out of the forty surveys sent out, thirty-one returned. Of this sample, ten (32 percent) relied solely on day-care facilities during their working hours. Twelve (39 percent) relied on family members. Of these, five were mothers-in-law and two were mothers who lived with the family. The other five were relatives who lived separately. Seven others (22.5 percent) relied on a combination of family members and day-care facilities. One person did not answer the question. Despite the controversy raging in the media over the problem of "latch key children" in dual career homes, only one respondent had no one to look after her two children, ages eleven and fourteen, when they came home from school.

Those who had their children in private centers thought that the tuition was too high. However, public centers fill up first, so many women have no choice but to resort to private centers. Even then, it can be difficult to find a center with space for the child, as in Koga san's case, below. Although Azumi people who had children in day care of any sort occasionally complained about the cost, I never heard anyone say anything negative about the treatment their children received there. All those in the survey indicated that they were satisfied with the day-care methods and environment. All the disapproving comments I heard came from those without children or those who had raised their children themselves until they were grown before reentering the work force. I did hear complaints from those who relied on grandparents; they said they spoiled the children.

Two of my coworkers with children in day care praised the care and education their children were receiving as superior even to that they would receive at their grandparents' hands. When I asked Fujii san why she did not leave her children with her mother rather than putting them in day care, she replied:

> If I left them with Mother, I'd have to pay her plus feel uncomfortable about it. She's getting on, and also I'd have to give her some pocket money. So I'd rather leave them at the day-care center where they can be carefree and play with other kids their own age. If it's Grandma, she'd tell them not to do this or that, and they wouldn't feel that they could do anything by themselves. At the day-care center they teach them about how to do things they didn't know they could do themselves. They learn a lot of things from group life. Sure day care is expensive,[5] but it has content.[6] At first I, too, thought it'd be a pity to put them into day care, inasmuch as Grandma and Grandpa are both around. But once I enrolled them, I found that in terms of [program] content, the value is greater [than leaving them with my parents]. I hadn't realized it. I feel that I was wrong [to worry].

Koga san's remarks concerning the day-care center were also favorable. She, too, had qualms about putting her children in day care, but now feels at ease, not only because they have made many friends, but also because there is nothing unusual about their situation now that so many women are working:

> When they were small I felt sorry for them putting them in the day-care center. But now that they're three or four, I think it was good I put them in. They made a lot of friends. Nowadays they all are in day care somewhere, right? Kindergartens, day care . . . so I don't think my kids are especially hurting. Since the older child will be going to school soon, it's too bad I won't be at home. But

since I've told them that I can't buy them things without money, they say, "It's OK for you to work."

She also had a positive view of the teaching at the day-care center:

> Since they have been in day care since they were infants, I haven't taught them anything at home. I have the day-care center teach them everything—from how to dress themselves to how to use the toilet. Or, at mealtimes, how to hold a spoon and so on. To me, this has been a great help. Once they reach age four, they can do just about everything by themselves. About the only thing they can't do is wipe themselves after a bowel movement. I am thankful to the day-care center.

After the expense, the greatest disadvantage of day-care centers is that the hours may be too short, especially if the worker needs to do overtime. In many households the husband returns home from work or *tsukiai* quite late each evening and cannot be relied upon to pick up the child from day care every day. Women whose relatives care for their children can manage overtime more easily, but for others it is a problem. At the center my daughter attended in 1990, I often saw grandparents picking up or dropping off the children, probably for this reason. Moreover, my coworkers complained that it was not easy to find a center with a vacancy. Koga san describes her efforts to find day care:

> K: When I got pregnant with my older child, eight months pregnant, we moved [to this apartment]. They won't do anything for you if you've already had the baby, see? So I went to the teacher and asked before the baby was born. I brought what I should have brought. I brought cakes. So, she said, "We'll look after the baby for you." But, unexpectedly, the teacher who said she'd look after the baby went on leave with back pains. But she went to the welfare office and asked them to do all they could to let us in. So we got in.
> G: You had connections.
> K: That's right. That's right. And it worked because it was just the time when the day-care center was opened. If it's a new place, they take a lot of people. If it's an already established place, they can't take in that many. So it worked out right.

On a return trip to Kyoto in 1990, I had an opportunity to experience Japanese day care centers firsthand. I placed my one-year, eight-month-old daughter in a public center. The hours were 8:30 to 5:45, Monday through Friday, and Saturdays as well for parents who had to work. The center cared for children from infants through age three. In some ways it was quite labor-intensive for the parents, especially mothers. We had to hand-sew numerous bags and covers to specification, and there was a load of laundry each night because the children did not wear diapers. The extra work sometimes exasperated me, but I also appreciated their meticulous care. For instance, each child had a notebook in which the mother or father was to write an account of what went on in the household after s/he had been picked up. For their part, the teachers kept records of how much the child had eaten, how long s/he had napped, what activities s/he had participated in and which s/he had particularly enjoyed, whether the child had had a bowel movement, and so on. The school had a nutritious hot lunch included in the monthly fee, and teachers took care to note children's eating habits. A public health doctor examined all children once a month, and parents were promptly informed if a child needed medical treatment.

The teachers were always eager to discuss the child's condition. There was a parent and teachers' meeting each month where parents (usually mothers) formed a circle and discussed their child's development, and shared their concerns. Teachers and other parents would join in with words of encouragement, offering solutions to problems, and so on. At this time teachers would also inform us of any changes in the curriculum. There were also occasional opportunities for parents to participate in the program for a half-day.

When the weather was fine the children were outdoors most of the time, engaged in all manner of activities. The children took a walk around the neighborhood every day, often to a temple grounds where they would play ghosts underneath the temple veranda. Or they might have a picnic on the Imperial Palace grounds, or visit the local fish market. The teachers, civil servants who were day-care professionals, used the hands-on approach. You could find them squatting in the sandbox, rolling on the floor singing songs, tossing a tot in the air, or comforting and cuddling. In the short three months we were there, my daughter made big strides in the language, called some of her classmates by name and was friends with them, knew when to bow in greeting or thanks, and was almost completely toilet-trained. She also lifted her arms and said *"Banzai!"* to take her T-shirts off.[7]

As a total outsider, I fared much better in my experience at this public center than did Fujita Mariko, a Japanese scholar and university professor who enrolled her one-and-a-half-year-old son in a Japanese day-care center in 1987 after their return from living in the United States. She writes of the disapprobrium she received from her neighbors because she was leaving her child in day care in order to carry out research, and of the difficulties she had with the overly critical attitudes of the personnel at her son's center and at other centers that she observed. (Fujita 1989). Other Japanese female researchers I know have had similar problems. That my coworkers at Azumi seemed to have no such problem may be evidence that day care in the 1980s, as it was earlier in Japanese history, is intended for working-class women rather than for intellectuals. On the other hand, scholars who put their children in day-care centers may also be less willing to leave everything up to the caretakers, as did the women I knew at Azumi, and this may cause friction.

Like my coworkers at Azumi, the working women I met through my daughter's day-care center were highly appreciative of the care their children received. With help from the older generation, day-care centers, and the school system, my coworkers could work with the assurance that their children were in good hands. After the workday ended, they went home to the busy job of household manager, wife, and mother. Who did the work of keeping the family fed, bathed, and clothed, the house clean and orderly? Are these full-time workers professional housewives as well? I shall now explore these questions.

# 9

# *Juggling Home and Work*

ONE DAY as I was taking a taxi to the train station, the driver and I struck up a conversation. I told him I was interviewing *paato* about their jobs and their homes, and asked him what he thought of the increase in married women workers. He replied with conviction that it was all right for women to work as long as they didn't let things slide at home. In fact, when his wife asked his permission to go out to work, he told her just that. He then bemoaned the present standard of consumption where everyone wants to be a homeowner and every family wants to send its children to college. He thought it would be far preferable to make do with less and enjoy life. His comments parallel those of some Azumi women we met in Chapter 1 who thought that people had become too extravagant. Whether or not his wife felt conflict over going out to work we cannot know. She may have shared the ambivalence of some Azumi women who wanted to keep up with the Tanakas yet wondered if this new life-style was worthwhile.

Why should this taxi driver have had such reservations about his spouse's employment? Wives in farm families have always been active in both agricultural and domestic activities.[1] The wives of self-employed entrepreneurs and professionals (doctors, dentists, etc.) who make up the ranks of "unpaid household workers," also contribute their energies to the business. This is expected of them as members of the household.[2] But over the past several decades, as Japan has urbanized and industrialized, a new niche has been created for the wives of salaried employees. It is that of professional housewife/manager, who oversees everything related to the household. With urbanization, most men could find nonagricultural jobs in the cities and establish their own nuclear families independent of their *ie* (main-stem family) back home. As Ueno (1987b:S79) explains, this meant that every married woman had the opportunity to become a *shufu,* the "main" woman of the household who, in stem families, had control over all subordinate female members of the household (daughters, unmarried sisters-in-law, daughters-in-law). The rural and merchant *shufu,* through their labor, also had a good deal of control over the household economy. Although she could have the title, however, a salaried man's wife does not have the power of the rural *shufu* and merchants' wives. Ueno notes that the title *okusan,* the term of address now used to refer to married women, originated in the late Meiji period. Literally meaning "lady in the back room," it first applied to the wives of samurai, and later to urban housewives. The taxi driver saw himself proudly as a salaried employee, able to support his wife and children on his own.

When I discussed the cabby's words with one of my Japanese friends, her explanation was insightful. She said that many men would rather make do with less income and keep their wives at home. That way, as the "pillar of the household" they can be proud sole supporters of their families. When a wife insists on working, such men believe that, as it is not really necessary that she also work, she is obliged to maintain the household as before.

Pride is not the only reason for a man's resistance to his wife getting a job. From interviews with my coworkers, I found that a husband's approval of his wife's working depends on several factors. These include his upbringing, his age, whether she has always worked, whether he regards her income as necessary, and whether there is someone at home or nearby, such as parents or in-laws, who are willing to help with the housework and child care.

## Dual-Income Household Management

Setting aside for a moment the question of whether a husband approves of his wife taking outside employment, let us consider the problem of household management in the absence of a full-time homemaker. From the cabby's account we can see that his wife's going out to work did not change his ideas about gender roles. He expected her to continue to maintain the household in the same way she always had. It is quite possible that she, too, held this expectation. According to a 1981 survey by the Cabinet Office, this attitude is commonplace in dual-income nuclear households. This survey amply illustrates that the lion's share of household maintenance is shouldered by wives in single- and dual-income families alike. In dual-income nuclear households, the wife gets thirty-four minutes less sleep and devotes three hours and thirty-one minutes more time to household chores and child minding than her husband. She also spends forty minutes less per day on leisure activities than he does. Her husband works at his job two and one-half hours longer than she.

What are the reasons behind Japanese men's lack of involvement in household chores? They may not have much time to spare. *Tsukiai* and/or overtime work are generally expected of male employees. The most important factor, however, is surely the influence of socialization. People who are brought up assuming a strict gender-based division of labor may find it difficult to alter this pattern, even if they recognize that it places a dual burden on the wife who takes on a job. The husband may feel incapable of doing household chores because of an upbringing that has excluded him from household participation. Also, taking out the garbage or cleaning the outside of the dwelling may subject him to loss of face with the neighbors.

The wife, raised in the same milieu, may share her husband's feelings of male incompetence in household work. She may feel uneasy about having her husband "invade" her domain of responsibility. Vogel (1963), Edwards (1987, 1989), Ueno (1987), and others view male/female role complementarity and sphere autonomy as a source of women's power in the Japanese household. Sharing work is sharing power. Perhaps the taxi driver's wife was as reluctant for him to interfere in the household sphere as he was himself. Yet, I wonder. Once she went out to work, was she quite as eager to keep strict control of household management? Many of my informants were not bound by a felt need to maintain separate spheres. Even those who did want to do it all and were proud of it found themselves negotiating support as the years wore on and their energy ebbed.

Younger men who had small children but no live-in relative tended to help their wives more with the child care, and the wives expected this. When I asked if she and her husband divided the child care, Fujii san remarked:

No, we do it together, but we don't divide it. We do it as we please
—if one prepares dinner, the other watches the kids, and so on. If
he says, "I'll do it today," then I say, "OK I'll watch the kids." The
older child can play on her own, but the younger one crawls
around so it's dangerous. That's how we do it—not in any special
way.

Koga san often remarked that she and her husband are equals who
share household and child-care chores. About household management
she replied: "I do cooking and the laundry. That's all I do. Dad, my
husband that is, puts the kids in the bath, spreads out the bedding,
does miscellaneous things for the kids, dresses them, that sort of
thing."

Nishitani san also received quite a bit of help from her husband.
What is particularly interesting and unusual about her account is that
her husband, as manager of a small factory near their apartment, had
enough leeway in his job to return home if anything needed attending
to, and if he could not do it himself, an employee would do it for him.
Moreover, his return at 5:00 P.M. each day was rare for a salaried
employee. Nishitani san's account of her evening, though, is typical of
the worker with small children in day care who was still taking child-
care time:

> N: I do the shopping on the way home. When I get home, I start
> the laundry. While the first load is in, I make the side dishes and
> then go put the second load in.[3] Then I finish preparing the meal
> and cool off the children's portion. Then I go pick up the kids.
> The bus brings them as far as the apartment. That's around 6:00.
> I get out [of work] at 4:10[4] and get home at 5:00 with the shop-
> ping done. So I have quite a lot of time and I'm flexible. By the
> time they're home, I'm ready to feed them and put them in the
> bath.
>
> G: When does your husband come home?
>
> N: 5:00 P.M. His factory is right next door. So at noon he gets
> the rice ready for me. When I get home, all I have to do is push the
> switch on the rice cooker. So it's very convenient. He comes home
> for lunch, so he doesn't need a *bentō* (box lunch)! He doesn't need
> lunch money, either. And he will eat up the leftovers for me. He'll
> get things ready for me to an extent. He helps me. So even if I put
> the laundry or bedding out [to air] on a gray day, I don't have to

worry. My husband can come home and take it in for me anytime. And if he's out on business and can't do it, somebody from the company would come in and do it for me. (Laughs) I don't have to worry about it.

Nishitani san asserted that children are the responsibility of both parents, not just of the mother alone: "I do most of the looking after them. But since we both work, he shares some of the chores with me. I have him look after them as well. Otherwise, I wouldn't be able to work. It's no good for one to have all the burden. What both of us made together, both of us take care of!"

I heard similar comments from many of the younger women. Although they do not expect a total sharing of household chores and child-caring duties, they do expect cooperation. None said that they would prefer their husbands not to meddle in the kitchen, as the professional housewives in Vogel's study (1978) did. Nor did any seem ashamed to accept their husbands' help in household tasks; in fact, they considered it their due.

Most women who lived with their mothers-in-law shared household chores with them. Shimizu san did the laundry, the after-meal clean-up, and the cleaning of her and her husband's room; her mother-in-law assumed responsibility for the shopping, cooking, and general cleaning. My impression is that in households where mothers-in-law are present, my coworkers' husbands did little or no housework or child care. Kamida *hanchō* seemed to do most of her household's work, even though her mother-in-law lived there. This may be due to the mother-in-law's advanced age.

> K: If it's a school day, I make lunches in the morning, then make breakfast, feed the kids, make miso soup, give it to them, and go. Also I boil water for tea. When I get home, I go shopping, make the evening meal, and clean up.
> G: Does your husband do housework?
> K: No. Not a bit. Not in the least!
> G: Would you like him to?
> K: When I'm tired, yes, I'd like him to help a bit. But since he's a man, there's nothing you can do about it. We sometimes have quite a fight over that, though! When I want to go to bed, and he comes home—at the earliest, it's around 10:30, I guess. Every day it's like that. Once I pick up, I have to do it all over again. [Her

husband messes up the house after he gets home.] I get mad about that. Sometimes we quarrel over it.

Another woman who lived with her in-laws remarked that her husband took absolutely no interest in caring for their three children as he knew his parents would watch them. She said: "I feel that since he's their father he ought to help rear them, but Japanese men haven't reached this level of consciousness yet. It seems most leave it up to the women."

Those women who did not work outside the home when their children were small did the housework and child care with little help from their husbands but were grateful for what assistance they did obtain. Nakanishi san said:

> N: I did all of it when they were little. My husband wasn't the type who dislikes kids, so during the holidays he'd look after them if they were crying. He'd also take them after he came home in the evening if they were crying and I was busy. But I always fed them and changed them. Now that he's a grandpa, he's a softy, and he makes them their bottles and changes diapers, but for me he never did that. He'd only hold them.
> G: Did you expect more?
> N: No, I didn't. I felt it was a woman's work.

Kushida san had two children, one of whom was chronically ill. She did *naishoku* (in-home piecework) for many years because she had to be available in case the child needed her. She said: "We didn't divide child care, but when we had to take the child to the doctor, it was usually at night, and my husband did it for me. I got his cooperation an awful lot. . . . If I'd been alone, I don't know how I ever would have raised [the boy]."

Perhaps the emphasis in the literature on white-collar salaried men's households has focused on one extreme pattern of the urban Japanese household, uniformly characterized by the *kyōiku mama* (education-mama) professional housewife, whose husband does little or nothing on the rare occasions he happens to be at home. Although my respondents were familiar with this type of household, they did not accept it wholly. Some rejected it altogether.

In general, working wives shoulder more of the burden of household chores and child care than do their husbands, and most expect to do so. In the child-care strategy survey, when I asked who stayed home with a sick child, only two out of thirty answered that the husband would absent himself from work, while three others indicated that this was a possibility. The rest said that they themselves would stay home (eight), that their mothers or others would stay home (ten), or that they, their mothers, or others would stay home (six). One said the child would stay home alone in bed. Yet, as we saw from the testimonies above, some husbands cooperate a great deal in child care. The responses from the survey confirm this. As for actual care, no one left it totally up to her husband, and only one out of thirty said her husband did more than she did. Sixteen (53 percent) said their husbands looked after the children's needs about half *(hanbun gurai mendō o miteiru);* twelve (40 percent) reported they looked after them only a little *(sukoshi dake mendō o miteiru);* one said he did not look after them at all *(mattaku mendō o minai).*

If we look at whether the women felt their husbands took an interest in child rearing, we can see that interest and participation are not necessarily synonymous. Out of thirty-one respondents, twenty (65 percent) said their husbands were fairly interested *(maa maa kanshin ga aru)* in child rearing *(ikuji),* while six (19 percent) said their husbands displayed a great deal of interest *(taihen kanshin ga aru).* Five (16 percent) reported their husbands had little interest *(amari kanshin ga nai).* None reported no interest. Of the twenty women who reported that their husbands were fairly interested, however, eight said they looked after the children only a little. I can merely speculate why these men were interested bystanders rather than active participants in rearing their children. I suspect it is a combination of acceptance of a more sideline caretaking role for male parents and job constraints.

Of the thirty respondents to the question "What is your opinion of your husband's attitude toward child rearing?" two (7 percent) reported they were very satisfied and sixteen (53 percent) were fairly satisfied. Ten (33 percent) admitted slight discontent, and two (7 percent) were very discontented. Of the latter, one reported that her husband took hardly any interest in child rearing and did not participate in the least, while the other reported little interest in child rearing and only a small amount of participation. Of the former, seven out of ten had husbands who participated only a little. Yet three of the somewhat discontented group had spouses who reportedly did 50 percent of the child rearing. Whether their discontent arose from the spouse's interference in the wife's realm or from disagreement over methods was not revealed by this simple questionnaire. Those two who were happiest, though, reported that their husbands participated either 50 percent or more than they did themselves.

## Opinions of Mothers' Outside Employment

What did my coworkers' families feel about having the mother take on outside employment? Although I did not interview families directly, I did ask my coworkers how their relatives felt about their employment.

Generally speaking, those husbands who felt that their wives' contributions were necessary to the household budget were supportive, but those who preferred their wives to remain at home, like the taxi driver I mentioned earlier, were uncooperative. In particular, they were pointedly more unsympathetic when their wives were tired.

Hanami san, who had been married for a few years but as yet had no children, commented: "My husband wishes I'd stay at home, even without kids. He does give his OK, however, since we just barely make living expenses as it is, with our combined salaries. Rent is expensive."

Nishitani san could not accept her husband's cooperation without guilt:

> He probably thinks I don't appreciate him. If on occasion I'm tired and can't do the housework, he doesn't say, "Do this" or "Do that." Even in regard to the children, if I say, "Boy, am I [too] tired [to cook] today!" he'll say, "Shall we eat out?" I think he probably doesn't like it. He probably thinks I have absolutely no appreciation of him. He seems to keep his feelings back.

Usui san's husband was also approving:

> U: He seems to take it OK because we can't make it on his salary alone. At first I promised that it would only be the first three years of our marriage, but we can't live in our present house—because we have two kids, and there's no space. So he's come to terms with it, I think.
> G: How about his mother?
> U: She says, "You're suited to work, so work!" Rather than stay

home . . . since I'm young, the only time you can work is when you're young. And if you quit the company and then go back to work again, even if the work is the same, the pay is much lower, right? So if I'm going to be doing the same job anyway, it's better to stay on at the same company. I feel we should cooperate with each other and do it this way.

Koga san, who stressed that without her salary the family couldn't make it, said:

K: It's a given [that I work].
G: He supports the idea?
K: Yes. Because he knows we couldn't make do if I quit. Sometimes I say, "It's only proper for a man to provide for his wife." I get lazy and he says, "Do such and such," because he doesn't want to do it. In those cases I say, "OK. OK then. I'll quit work, and you support me." Then he says, "It's a matter of course that you work" (i.e., "Come on now!").

Hasegawa san's remarks indicated that work plus household responsibilities put stress on her, which she unloads on her family:

H: He [my husband] thinks that women turn into loudmouths when they work. Because you get tired—after work. It'd be great if I could listen and do whatever he tells me to, saying "Yes, yes," but I go and say, "But I'm so tired already!" Therefore, he probably is somewhat unhappy about it. But since I'm making money for us . . . he's quiet about it. But when women work, they always get uppity.
G: What about your kids?
H: Hmmm . . . they say I yell too much. I get mad. They say if I were taking it easy at home I wouldn't get mad. Naturally, when they make demands on me in spite of the fact that I come home tired out, I end up just saying whatever I feel like off the top of my head.

Fujii san's husband shared many of the domestic chores. Although she apparently got little verbal encouragement from him, she felt that actually he approved of her working:

G: Is he supportive?
F: Not especially.

G: Does he complain?

F: No, he doesn't. If I say I'm tired or I'm busy, he always says, "If you're tired, then why don't you quit?" But he's just saying that. He doesn't really mean it. I guess he thinks if I want to work, then it's OK by him.

Her children, however, are a source of encouragement:

G: How about the kids?

F: They don't say anything much. But when they say they don't like going to day care, I say, "Mother is going to go to work and do her best, so you do your best, too!" and we spur each other on, each going to work or day care. If you work, it becomes an encouragement to them, it seems. If you're just at home lazily looking after the kids, neither mother nor child grows. Because your knowledge is limited—what can one parent can teach a child? But at nursery school, many different teachers with varied knowledge teach the children all sorts of things—more than a parent teaches. So parents aren't quite as good. They end up having a lot of teachers, but I think that's good for the children.

Kamida *hanchō*'s husband is unsupportive, although he had agreed to her continuing work at the time of their marriage. Her children, however, give her understanding and help:

K: If I bring home my troubles when I'm tired, he tells me to quit. In our case, I'm working because I like to, not because there's any special [financial] difficulty. I want to work, so I do, but if I say anything, he says, "Then quit and be done with it." So I don't bring that up at home. I don't mention that I'm tired, and I don't bring up my gripes. Therefore, I don't talk about company matters at all. . . . Because he says such things . . . [I don't tell him about work].

G: How about the children?

K: They understand. I do things for them. It wouldn't do for people to talk about them because they have a working mother, so I do my best to wash their clothes. If I had them wear anything dirty they'd be talked about—so I have them wear clean things, and on vacations I take them places, since usually I'm not around.

G: Do you have them do any housework?

K: Sometimes I have them help. The older one is very nice and does anything. She spreads out the bedding for Grandma, and so on. Today she did my hair, you see? With the dryer. She's so nice. That's why everyone comments on how gentle they've been brought up to be. Despite my working. After all, they were left to themselves. I guess the kids know that, since their parents are working, they have to be responsible. So I guess they have an independence about them already. They even say I needn't come and watch their classes anymore, since I have to take off time from work.

Note the sense of responsibility Kamida san felt toward her children and her sensitivity to public opinion. In order to make sure they did not suffer from her working, she made an extra effort to keep her children in clean clothes and to take them places on holidays. She also remarked that when she served on the P.T.A., she received much praise for her good attendance record despite being a working mother.

Some women who reentered the work force after spending child-rearing years at home felt guilty about their return to work. Especially if something went wrong with a child, the woman tended to blame herself for having neglected him. Ogawa san's case is revealing:

O: They think there's nothing to be done about it.

G: In the beginning they didn't say anything?

O: Well, buying a house was why I went to work. So I had to work. The children knew it. The older one was a fifth-grader and the younger was a second-grader. They were pretty understanding and did things around the house for me. So they didn't object to my working. But my older child—that was just about the time when he was beginning to make his own judgments and become independent. I think he must have been lonesome for a while. I had him babysit for his younger brother during the summer and winter vacations. I had him take him roller skating . . . and he had to look after him in Boy Scouts. That was a big burden on the elder child, and after he started middle school, for a while he ran off the track. I guess I didn't give him enough love . . . I think now he was lonely then. Since I had him take care of the younger one. I haven't actually told him, but I think it was bad of me.

In some cases, husbands who had not shared household chores before helped out once their wives reentered the work force. Nakanishi san, like many older women, secured the "permission" of her husband and family before going out to work after many years at home. At first she managed the household single-handedly, but as she grew older this became more difficult to accomplish. Although she said that she felt guilty about the help she received from her husband, I could also sense that she was touched that her husband had recognized her contributions to the family and had made efforts to take some of the burden off her. In her words:

N: He suffers, I guess. Because I cause him so much trouble. Because I have him cooperate. He doesn't say it, but. . . .
G: Was it that way from the start?
N: No, the first two or three years . . . since I was still young, and since it was under the condition that I not inconvenience them that I had [selfishly] gotten their permission to leave the house, [I managed by myself]. I was getting on in years, but I was much younger than I am now, and I had strength, so I did almost everything by myself. But the older I get, the more worn out I get, and I put quite a burden on them. Because the fatigue builds up. I want this and that done for me. Even if I don't say anything, my husband can't help but notice, and often is the first to start cleaning up—washing cups, and the like. I'll say I'm tired and I just want to lie down and watch TV for a few minutes. But then I fall asleep and sometimes when I wake up, I find the dishes all washed and put away. So I'm causing a lot of trouble . . . I'm a burden.
G: What do the kids think?
N: I never really heard them say anything . . . but once in a while they do say I'm quite something. I go to work, and at night do the things—meals, wash, cleaning—that other mothers do during the day. I think they respect that, and they think I'm great for it. They seem to be quite thankful. My boy always says thank you when I do something for him. That makes me happy. He doesn't take me for granted. He always thanks me for doing what he requests. I think he's a dear.

Nakanishi san's attitude toward her role as a wife and mother contrasts sharply with that of the young mothers I have mentioned previously. When she gets help from her family, she is grateful and feels a bit guilty, for she does not share the younger women's notion that husbands' and wives' roles should overlap. Still, she felt the weight of her double shift at the end of the week:

> I don't notice it at all when I'm not tired, but as the weekend draws near, I get tired. And then I see that my husband leaves after 8:00 A.M., and when he comes home he says he is tired and he sits down. I work the same hours as he does, but there's no sitting for housewives when they come home. A housewife's work begins then. At those times I think it's unfair.

I heard this sort of comment repeatedly. In Nakanishi san's case, her husband did eventually share some of the housework, thus modifiying the pact she had made with the family when she first went out to work. However, not all husbands are willing to make many concessions, and some refuse to make any at all. The less cooperative the spouse, the more trouble occurs at home, and the more difficult the balancing act becomes. Doi *kachō* remarked that most women bring bad feelings from family quarrels to work, and this is a big problem for him. When I asked him if working in a division that has many women makes a difference in the atmosphere there, he replied:

> D: Naturally it does. And it differs with age. The relationship between home and work differs depending on the home environment. Of course they should have nothing to do with each other, but it is terribly difficult to balance home and work.
> G: How? Can you give an example?
> D: If the husband is a *teishu kanpaku* [ruler of the roost], and now the wife is out working as well, they both come home tired from work—and it's the same condition, since they're both working in factories—if the husband won't cover any of the housework for her, that doesn't come off well. The atmosphere at home . . . the relationship between husband and wife gets very difficult. She can't get him to cooperate. So when she comes to the company, that comes out in her work—she can't get rid of it. Business and home life—she can't keep them separate.

For men, whose traditional role requires them to be breadwinners for the family but asks very little of them in terms of household duties, conflict between home and work is minimal. Most women must balance both, however, if they are to be successful. Particularly in Japan, where sharp lines are drawn between private and public life, the woman who cannot clearly separate home and work will not be successful at either, and may be the object of criticism from family and/or coworkers. Matsumura *hanchō,* who is still hoping to marry one day, was sharply critical of working housewives who complain about their husbands' lack of cooperation. She had remarked earlier that if women were more frugal, most could get by on their husbands' salaries alone, and that extravagance is the root of their insistence on working. Indeed, her views and those of the taxi driver are remarkably similar. I knew that she disapproved of *amae* behavior at work. She also scorned women workers for *amae* behavior at home. She observed:

> You hear a lot lately that men are weak. Well, when women work, they get tired. They have to look after the kids, and when the husband gets home, even the wives who get help from their husbands complain about having to cook and so on. These housewives are spoiled, you could say. Women often tell me things like, "I can't do overtime because I'm a housewife," or "Isn't it easy for you [since you're not married]." But I think if that's how they feel, they shouldn't have gotten married. Since you get married because you feel happy—because there is something good that happened—you should take pride and tell the people who aren't yet married what a wonderful thing marriage is. I think it's weird when people say, "You'll get tired out if you marry" or "You'll have to do so many things." If you're working in order to help out your husband, you ought to be more cheerful about it. "My husband's salary is too small and so I have to work"—I think that saying something like that is disgraceful.

## Coming Together

Although a woman's going out to work can cause contention within the family, particularly between spouses, in some cases it can draw them together, as the wife comes to understand more about her husband's position in the workplace. Nakanishi san said that once she went out to work she stopped criticizing her husband for going out on so many *tsukiai,* because she learned how important they are. Moreover, she also learned to loosen up a bit and enjoy what leisure time she had. The way she chose to relieve stress was *pachinko*,[5] her husband's favorite pastime, which she had always despised—partly because it kept him away from home, and partly because she thought it slightly disreputable. Once she started working, she began to go to the parlor along with him, and eventually even by herself. She relates:

> N: I used to hate it [*pachinko*]. Now I go once in a while. My husband used to love it, but I had the children and wouldn't do such things until they grew up and went into society.[6] But first of all, I hated it. Sometimes I had to go there to get my husband. Even at those times, I didn't like even to set foot inside. I really hated it. We fought a lot about it. But someone told me they felt sorry for him—he was just going to play *pachinko,* after all, and not somewhere worse—and I realized that was so, and that I knew where he was and could go there if I had something to tell him. But one or two years ago I started going myself a bit. I've become a bit loose [*furyō*]! But just working isn't any fun and I think it's important to relieve stress. It's best the day before a holiday. At one point I went a lot—every day. Around 9:00 P.M. My husband would say, "Let's go!" and even if I said I was tired and wanted to stay home, he'd say "Let's go, let's go!" But lately, I go two or three times a month. I've even gotten to the point where I go by myself. I've changed, haven't I?!! I've become a no-good!
>
> G: No, no! (laughing).
>
> N: My daughter says I have. But she also says I'm cute.

From looking at the national statistics on men's participation in household chores one might conclude that a man who lends a helping hand in the domestic sphere is indeed a rarity. Among my coworkers there were those with husbands who fitted this pattern, but there were also not a few who actively contributed to household activities, especially child care, cooking, and dishwashing. Whether through explicit negotiation or tacit understanding gained over years of married life, those of my coworkers without live-in mothers-in-law had spouses who "helped out" at home. Such help undoubtedly made staying on the line much more of a likelihood.

# Conclusion

MANY OF THE issues I have raised in the preceding pages surely sound familiar to U.S. readers, and indeed, to readers in all economically developed countries. Whether impelled by rising costs, a desire for a higher living standard, or a desire to expand one's sphere of knowledge, influence, and expertise beyond the household, increasingly women are working as salaried employees throughout their adult lives. Concerns about how one is to manage both the "first shift" of the work world as well as the "second shift" of home chores (Hochschild 1990), how this trend will affect one's children, one's marriage, and one's health—such worries are shared by many if not most women who take on paid employment in addition to their household responsibilities.

The women at Azumi were loyal to their company and openly proud of its accomplishments. They were willing to adjust their pace or schedule to the company's needs. Most were outwardly acquiescent to authority, although they were certainly not passive or uncritical. They also had a stake in the company, through the bonus system. There was another sense in which they had a stake in the company: they had few choices. Azumi women were unlikely to find jobs with comparable wages and benefits if they quit. Far from a step out being a step up, as is often the case in the United States, once having quit, the only recourse for most women would have been to become a *paato,* even if the hours were full-time. Few firms hire mid-level-entry women as regular employees nowadays. This was common knowledge, and this surely tempered Azumi women's reactions to problems with job conditions.

Compared to women in the United States, my Azumi coworkers lacked assertiveness in pressuring the company to open access to higher-paying, higher-ranked jobs for them. One reason for this may well be that the majority of married women I knew were in stable marriages. Their partners had regular jobs and their families assumed that they would remain in them. My coworkers certainly did not anticipate a time when they might have to support themselves and their children on their own. While I was at Azumi, the husband of one of the Health Section nurses died unexpectedly. She was left with three children to raise. I remember her dismay when she assessed her situation. She remarked that it was going to be very difficult to make a living for all of them, especially in the unwelcoming atmosphere the company provided. One reason why Fujii san was so eager to try for promotions when the opportunity arose may have been that she knew that she, too, might someday face this situation, because her husband had a serious chronic illness. When I asked my college-educated professional housewife friends what they would do if they became widowed or divorced, they said they prepared for it by taking out multiple insurance policies, as they knew they could not support a family on any job they would be likely to obtain.

Another reason for this lack of assertiveness for promotion is the strict working standard we have discussed. My coworkers knew the high standard, and most of them did not aspire to commit themselves to the extent necessary to attain it. It would have meant more curtailing of family life, even less personal time. Few felt it was worth it. Interestingly enough, opinion polls in the past few years have shown that young Japanese men and women (called *shinjinrui,* "the new breed") are more interested in leisure and personal time, and indicate an unwillingness to devote themselves to company life to the extent of their elders. If they persist in this attitude and carry it into the workplace, perhaps this will relax the standard a bit, making it easier for the woman who wishes to have both a career and a family.

These blue-collar women were bucking the system. They knew the value of their work, but most were hard put to get others—whether company management, husbands, or in-laws—to acknowledge it. Children seemed to offer the most support and gratitude.

The system is in transition, however, and may offer women

employees more alternatives and more welcoming conditions in the coming decades. Since I left Azumi in the summer of 1985, some changes have taken place. Fujii san says that women are being given more encouragement to take promotional exams. She herself has successfully passed two, and now uses computers to monitor inventory. On the other hand, women are required to do some of the heavy work, such as lifting boxes. The older women have a hard time with this, but they have stuck it out anyway. Taniguchi san, the disabled woman who hoped for her "rock-solid" pension at retirement, is now actually nearing it. The company has instituted a program whereby employees can retire five years early without penalty, and she plans to take advantage of it. Hasegawa san, the feisty coworker who fought so hard for her vacation days, will take full retirement in one more year. She is already planning her trip to Hawaii. Nakanishi san, the *pachinko* fan whose husband gradually began to help with household chores, and Ogawa san, are also still there. The two young *shisutaa*, though, have both married and left, having run up against problems of balancing motherhood with work. Yamamoto san also left, tired of the job after spending her youth at it. Murakami *kakarichō* has not yet quit to set up the restaurant she hoped to manage, nor has Matsumura *hanchō* fulfilled her dream of leaving to become a kindergarten teacher or day-care center aide. In a recent (1990) telephone conversation, Fujii san estimated that about half of the women who transferred from the factory to the shipping center are still working there. One major change is that employees now have a two-day weekend. The Ministry of Labor has been pushing firms to shorten the workweek, and now Azumi has taken the step. Fujii san hastened to note that in exchange for having weekends free, employees now have to work on holidays.

What is the government's vision for women's employment? Far from Azumi's floor, intellectuals, Japanese officialdom, and labor and management representatives began thrashing out this issue when the government ratified the U.N. Convention concerning the Elimination of All Forms of Discrimination against Women, in 1980.

Let me provide an example of what one intellectual, Hasegawa Michiko (1984), had to say about equal employment opportunities for women. She suggested that any system has its costs, and that the cost of Japan's employment system is the difficulty women have in gaining access to equal opportunity. This price is worth paying, she argued, because it keeps the family intact. If women were to work as men do, she warned, the family would fall apart. In any case, Japanese culture assigns housewives a high status, so what is wrong with a separate-but-equal, interdependent division of labor?

This line of thought is reminiscent of the anniversary speech of Azumi's president. He saw women as spiritually strong, the backbone of the household, even stronger than men—as long as they remain true to their callings as wives and mothers. What is wrong with a system that requires the separation of spheres, as long as partners respect each other and find meaning within their respective realms? Why should we give equal employment opportunity to women, asked Hasegawa, when housewives are quite content with the system as it is? To draw an analogy, why should one take medicine when one is not ill? The to-do over employment opportunities, she insisted, is rooted in Japan's sensitivity to Western opinion, not in any indigenous cultural malaise.

Many of my coworkers would find points of agreement with Hasegawa. They were proud to be wives and mothers. But they were also proud to be workers supporting their families. Many felt that the treatment they faced at work was inevitable if their husbands were to have stable, well-remunerated positions, so they put up with it. When the EEOA (Equal Employment Opportunity Act) began to be discussed in the media, from about 1983 on, few of my coworkers paid attention to the debate. They did not feel it would have much impact on their daily situation.

Where my coworkers would disagree with Hasegawa is on the importance of their employment to the well-being of their households. Although not asking to be on the fast track, nor wishing for jobs which entail long hours of overtime or transfer to distant locations, they would have liked a greater measure of job assurance.

I doubt, however, that most blue-collar women workers would seek equal opportunity in the workplace if it meant equal in every way to the conditions men now enjoy. Does this mean they would be happy to stay home? I think not. Although there is no rising tide of feminism, ideas about women's role in the household and in society are changing. If Japan's employment system grants more equality to women workers, it will be based on cultural ideas that recognize women and men as intrinsically different and make provisions for women workers that allow them to be mothers as well as workers.

This kind of vision for Japan's future can be seen in the writings of

Sakamoto Fukuko (1989) and Honda Junryo (1986), among others. Sakamoto urged a "humanizing" of the workplace, wherein both men and women regular employees would have shorter hours, less overtime, and more vacations. Job transfers to distant locations would be subject to an employee's circumstances. Changes such as these would give married women a chance to compete for career jobs. A one-year leave after childbirth and leaves for taking care of sick family members without job loss would also be provided, and facilities for child care with more accommodating hours would be increased. More nursing homes for the elderly would also need to be built to better secure women's long-term attachment to the labor force. She envisioned a balanced family and work life, wherein men, freed from the all-consuming company life, would have the time to participate fully in the household along with their wives.

In different ways, both Hasegawa and Sakamoto present idealized views, and the distance between their stances speaks volumes about the lack of consensus on this issue. Whereas Hasegawa underestimated the changes taking place in women's conception of their roles, Sakamoto overestimated the likelihood that men, given the opportunity to spend more time off the job, would choose to devote it to sharing their wives' sphere. Indeed, would all wives want them to? Moreover, when a large firm like Azumi finally agreed to conform to the Ministry of Labor's two-day weekend mandate, they made up for much of the time lost by requiring holiday work. How likely is it that companies will be convinced to shorten work hours further, and to give generous leaves of absence for childcare or care of the elderly? If large firms are reluctant to make such changes, how much more so will be small and medium-sized firms operating on much smaller profit margins. Yet Sakamoto's vision of an employment arena that recognizes the importance of the family and accommodates women's role in it is perhaps the only route whereby significant numbers of Japanese women could achieve "equality" in employment.

Those who agree with Sakamoto and Honda think that Japan, as a major world power, ought to be able to afford to make such changes. They point to EEC countries like Sweden that have generous parental leave policies and much shorter work hours and ask: Why not us? Who can afford this better than Japan? If one could base the answer on financial resources alone, it would surely be "No one." But economic systems are not free from cultural ideas about the construction of gender, and these, rather than wealth, are at the root of the issue.

After much debate, in 1985 the Diet passed the Equal Employment Opportunity Act, effective April 1, 1986. This law requires employers to "endeavor" to give equal opportunity and treatment to men and women in the areas of recruitment and hiring, job assignment and promotion, and education and training. They are prohibited from discriminating against women on the basis of sex in the areas of employee benefits, mandatory retirement age, retirement, and dismissal.

No penalties are levied upon firms that do not "endeavor" to follow the law. Instead, the law calls for firm-based dispute resolution forums. If resolution fails, a case can be brought to the director of the prefectural Ministry of Labor Offices of Women's and Young Workers' Affairs. If this fails, mediation by a prefectural Equal Opportunity Mediation Commission is possible, if both parties agree to it (EEOA, Article 13, in Parkinson 1989:607).

With the enactment of the EEOA, the Labor Standards Law was also revised, weakening some protective measures for women workers. For instance, the right to take menstruation leave was rescinded, except in especially severe cases. People on the management side of the debate pointed to menstruation leave as an archaic provision deserving abolishment. Labor representatives, on the other hand, felt that the leave should be retained to protect women's health.

Management representatives also pushed to have overtime restrictions abolished, arguing that restrictions on overtime and late-night work for women also act only to hinder women's advancement in employment. With the EEOA, the two hours per day, six hours per week limitation on overtime for factory women has been changed to lift the daily limit. Now factory women workers could be asked to work up to six hours of overtime in one day, as long as they did no other overtime that week. Women who work in office, sales, and service industries have had overtime restrictions lightened to twenty-four hours a month (no weekly limit) or 150 hours a year. Unlike factory workers, they may be asked to work one holiday every four weeks (Miyaji and Honda 1986:25).

The reader might wonder why women should be entitled to special protections. The United States has interpreted equality in employment quite differently, and has not made legal provisions that accommodate women's role as potential child bearers and rearers. In Japan, labor's position is that such provisions are necessary in order for ordinary women to maintain regular jobs and households simultaneously. If women were expected to work the long hours and quantity of overtime that is the norm for men, they argue, they would never be able to maintain their health, their jobs, and their households (Ishii Ayako 1985).

Maternity leave was strengthened after the EEOA. It was extended by two weeks to a total of fourteen weeks. Furthermore, the EEOA encouraged firms to grant year-long leaves of absence after maternity leave, with the opportunity to return to one's former status. If this becomes common practice it will have an enormously positive effect on women's ability to build careers in the work force.

How has this law actually affected working women? Have blue-collar women been affected differently from white-collars? At the time of its passage, labor representatives and left-wing lawyers cum social reformers felt that it gave up too many protections without offering concrete gains. They also feared that it was skewed favorably toward the well-educated elite, career-women workers, while undermining the position of their blue- and pink-collar counterparts. For the latter, removal of overtime and night-work protections might mean they would be forced out of regular employee positions. That is to say, companies that desired regular-status women to quit could force their hands by requiring them to work more overtime and/or do night work. For women who are just barely able to meet the demands of the normal workday schedule, such requirements could mean the end of their careers as regular employees. The underlying presumption is that women need these protections to allow them to perform the dual role of regular-status worker and homemaker/mother. While elite women workers need freedom from protections in order to compete with men on an equal basis, others who work in physically taxing jobs need legal protections in order to maintain their regular employee status. If men's jobs were less time-consuming and if men participated equally in household chores, then such protections would be unnecessary. It is still early to assess the full impact of the EEOA on blue-collar women.

Upham (1987) argues that through the enactment of the EEOA, the government successfully maneuvered the equal opportunity arena out of the courts and into its own hands. This would allow it, more than the courts, to control the pace and quality of change. Parkinson

(1989) sees the legislation as a brilliant compromise, the perfect solution to a highly charged political issue. With the EEOA, she asserts, a gradual and voluntaristic change can occur through persuasion. As women prove themselves worthy employees, firms will open their doors to them with ever-increasing willingness. She suggests that in the areas of gender discrimination and civil rights, the United States might learn from Japan's noncoercive, mediational approach.

Having experienced the atmosphere of company life at Azumi, I am skeptical of how effective firm-based mediation would be. Would women feel confident enough in the system to approach a complaint board within their own companies? Would such boards hear their claims impartially? Granted, mediation has had a long history of success in Japan. But whether it is appropriate in cases where the parties are on patently unequal grounds is questionable. While some firms are taking the new law seriously, one factory manager told me that the EEOA is Japan's *tatemae* (window dressing) for the world.

Certainly not all Japanese regard the law as mere window dressing. Bureaucrats with whom I spoke in 1985 regarded it as a step toward more equal working conditions for women. Yet while the government passed this law, they have backed off from passing a law that would give *paato* better conditions. The LDP has strong backing from the conservative sectors of the society, which ultimately seem ill-at-ease with working housewives. Married working women are welcome only as *paato*, or at-home pieceworkers, who, as tax dependents of their husbands, still fall under the housewife rubric, yet who fuel the economy with their cheap labor. These women raise their children well and keep the elderly from lonely ends in nursing homes. Thanks to them, the Japanese economy has flourished, while the family, although not unaffected by modernization, has maintained a level of stability surprising in a society that has seen so much change.

Besides the gentle proddings of the Labor Ministry, demographics may push firms to create employment conditions more suitable to women. In a study of human resource management and corporate strategy in banks and insurance companies, the OECD reported that although the three Japanese banks in their study had initially responded to the EEOA by circumventing it, one year later, in 1987, two of them had "taken steps" toward equal opportunity. The reasons given for this were two. The first was structural. With a rapidly aging population, Japanese employers are beginning to feel a labor crunch.

If they continue to marginalize their female labor force, they will find themselves short-handed. The second reason was cultural. Firms must increasingly deal with "the rising tide of the new generation of college-educated women less and less content with the roles in which their elders were once confined" (OECD 1988:80).

As we saw at Azumi, discontent with a role that excludes employment for married women is not confined to college-educated women, nor necessarily to young women. The numbers of women in the work force at all points of the life cycle belie the image of the household with a salaried man and a professional housewife. Certainly this image did not hold true for Azumi's women, and it is rapidly becoming less true for women of all class backgrounds, as they turn to *paato* work after their children are in school. In her finely crafted book on Japanese women's roles in the economy, Mary Brinton states: "Change in Japan will mainly be produced by the economic necessity for employers to hire and keep good workers. In the decades to come more and more of these workers will be women" (1993:238).

Whether companies will prefer to demarginalize the female labor force or turn to more-than-willing senior citizens, immigrants, or off-shore labor remains unknown. In any case, the increasing numbers of women like those at Azumi, determined to "stay on the line" for as long as possible, may gradually redraw the M-curve and make the Japanese business environment more amenable to women workers.

# Appendix: Interview Questions

1. What is your name?
2. What is your age?
3. Are you married?
4. What is your husband's job?
5. What was your last year of schooling?
6. Where do you live?
7. What work do you do in your company?
8. Did you have any special training in order to get this job?
9. Are you a regular employee?
10. When did you start working here?
11. Do you plan to work until retirement? At this workplace?
12. What do you like most about your job?
13. What do you like least?
14. When looking for a job, what do you consider most important?
15. Have you ever done overtime? What do you think of it?
16. Do you have people whom you get along well with at work?

17. Do you associate with them after hours?

18. Have you ever held more than one job at once? What about in-home piecework?

19. Is your present workplace easy to work at? How are personal relationships?

20. If there are any problems at your workplace, what are they?

21. When problems come up at work, what do you do?

22. With whom do you talk over your worries about work?

23. Which is better, a male or female supervisor?

24. Are you in the union? How does it help you?

25. What sort of woman is the typical woman worker, in your opinion? What is your image of her?

26. Do you think there is work that only women can do or that women are better suited for? How about work that only men can do or are better suited for?

27. Before you married, did you plan to work after marriage?

28. How do you use your income?

29. Who holds the purse strings in your family?

30. Do you have children? How old are they?

31. How do you raise the children? Who takes care of them?

32. When the children are sick, what do you do?

33. How do you do housework?

34. What does your husband think of your working? Your children? Your parents/in-laws?

35. Do you think that there's a difference in male/female work conditions? What do you think about that?

36. Do you think men and women should get equal pay for equal work?

37. Is work as important to a woman as it is to a man? How about the motivation to work—is it the same?

38. What's your opinion of the professional housewife?

39. What do you think of the saying "Men should work outside and women should keep the home"?

40. If a man and woman have the same ability and work at the same place, and one of them has to be laid off temporarily, who should be laid off?

41. What do you think is the reason for the increasing number of women workers in the past ten years? Do you think there will be any influence on society because of it? How about husband/wife relations or parent/child relations? (Will they change?)

42. What are your plans after retirement? Your hopes for the future?

43. What is your opinion of the proposed changes in the regulations of the Labor Standards Law? Do you think you need menstruation leave? Should overtime restrictions for women be lifted? What about restrictions on nighttime work?

44. My questions are over, but if you have anything to add, please go right ahead.

# Notes

## Introduction

1. *Ryōsai kenbo* is a slogan representing the Japanese version of Catherine Beecher's late-nineteenth-century cult of female domesticity. It located woman's sphere in the household and defined her mission as the education of children and complete devotion to her husband, supporting him in his role as a productive member of the work force. Unlike the American-bred ideology, which grounded its rationale for self-sacrifice and domesticity on a concept of romantic conjugal love, *ryōsai kenbo* was based on the concept of loyalty to the *ie* (stem-family descent line), the emperor, and the state. For a discussion of the cult of domesticity in the United States, see Sklar (1973); Sievers (1981) discusses its emergence in Japan.

2. I refer to Japan's part-time workers using their term, *paato* (derived from the English), so as not to confuse their meaning with ours. *Paato* work does not necessarily entail shorter hours than those of an employee of regular status. Indeed, many manufacturing *paato* work as many hours as their regular-employee counterparts. The difference lies in benefits, wages, and job security, which are vastly inferior to those of regular employees.

3. Like many lingerie companies in Japan, Azumi had its own sales force, which it trained to sell its product line exclusively in Azumi boutique sections of department stores as well as in separate Azumi shops. The salesladies were Azumi employees, but their working hours conformed to those of the stores where they were employed.

## 1 Azumi's Good Wives and Wise Mothers

1. My impression is that this does not pertain to upper-income families, where women who are full-time housewives often engage in extradomestic activities such as tennis, tea ceremony, cultural center classes, and so on.

2. This teacher/student relationship strikes me as similar to the position of the *nakōdo* (go-between) and the married couple. If something goes wrong in the marriage, the *nakōdo* is expected to try to patch it up and encourage the bride to try harder to make the marriage work. The underlying message in both cases is that nothing worthwhile is easy to attain. The road to maturity and fulfillment is the world of hard knocks; the individual must not give up, must do her best to overcome all difficulties.

3. In August 1990, the topic of women's changing roles and their implication for Japan's future came under national scrutiny again when the media took up the problem of the low birthrate.

4. Since 1986, the company has asked several younger women (under 40) including Fujii san, to enter a training program for the next promotional level and to take the test upon completion of the program. Fujii san passed and has since learned the duties of her new post, which requires office skills and ability to input data into a computer. In 1988 she was asked to test for the next higher credentialed level, *fukushūji*. She was thrilled to be included among those considered for promotion. She said about one-fourth of those testing at this level were female employees. Another factor that encouraged the company to invest in Fujii san is her family circumstances. Her husband is chronically ill, and the firm knows that Fujii san intends to continue her job until retirement at age sixty.

## 2 The Daily Challenge: Cope or Quit?

1. I had never encountered *hansei* before, and when I asked the women at the factory where the practice had come from, they replied that it was peculiar to Murakami *kakarichō* and not to Azumi. Since then, from a conversation with Takie Lebra I have learned that the practice of *hansei* was quite common in pre–World War II schools as a means of making children reflect on their bad behavior. It has fallen from favor as standard practice in postwar education, although some teachers still use it. Japanese informants have told me that *hansei* is also a feature of the new religions. It is also used in sports teams and other clubs, but more often as a group technique, where each member reflects on how his performance could be improved, rather than the individual, more punitive style of Murakami *kakarichō*. Merry White, in *The Japanese Educational Challenge: A Commitment to Children* (1987:32), notes the improvement orientation of *hansei*: "A child is encouraged to practice such examination to seek out his own sources of weakness, self-discovery being much better than having others point out flaws in character."

2. In January 1984, Murakami *kakarichō* was transferred to the Sewing Division, and we had an interim male *kakarichō* until we moved to the shipping center in April. The farewell party to which Ogawa san refers is the one we held for Murakami san.

3. This act was a symbolic expulsion of Kinami san from the community of the I&P. In Japan, when mothers are particularly angry with their children, one of the most severe punishments is to lock the misbehaving child out of the house for a time (Lebra 1976:151).

4. Clark (1979:154) categorizes employees by their ability and/or willingness to change employers. "Immobile" employees are: older women (presumably, he notes, in family firms); older men, especially in large firms; and graduates. "Mobile" employees are young women, younger, less-educated men, and temporary and irregular employees who have a weak association with any particular employer.

### 3 A Lifetime of Line Work: Making It to Sixty

1. The factory manager told me that roughly one-third quit at marriage, one-third at pregnancy, and one-third for "personal reasons."

2. For an interesting documentary report on the effects of employee transfer on salaried men's wives, see Saito Shigeo, *Tsumatachi no Shishūki* (Tokyo: Kyōdōtsūshinsha, 1983).

3. One example is the case of *Higuchi v. the Asahi Fire Casualty Marine Corporation (Asahi Kasai Kaijō Hoken Kabushikigaisha)*. On September 12, 1986, Mr. Higuchi sued his employer, Asahi Kasai, for unfairness in ordering him to transfer from his job at the Kobe branch office to an office with only seven employees in Kanagawa. His suit was fought on two grounds: first, that the order to transfer was an unfair labor practice because it was a move down rather than a promotion, intended to thwart his union activities and make him quit. In such posts as secretary of the Osaka District Council and chairman of the Asahi branch of the Kobe chapter, he had been very active in the All Japan Casualty Insurance Labor Union (Zen Nippon Songai Hoken Rōdō Kumiai), which had strongly opposed company efforts to rationalize operations beginning in 1978. From 1980 the management intervened in labor-union elections at all levels, supporting those who did not resist the rationalization efforts. By 1981 they were successful in ridding the executive union ranks of all members who had opposed rationalization. At the time of the order to transfer, the union chapter of which Higuchi was a member was the only remaining chapter having three posts filled by those opposing the rationalization tactics, Higuchi being the central one. Hence, by transferring Higuchi to Kanazawa, the company apparently sought to remove an employee who was a thorn in its side.

The second ground on which Higuchi fought was that the company had no right to force an employee to accept a transfer that entailed separation from his family, and hence suffering and disruption of family life. His wife, who had held a job in another insurance company in Osaka for twenty-two years, and their three children, could not accompany him to the new assignment.

The Kobe District Court found in favor of Higuchi san, ordering Asahi Fire & Marine to rescind the transfer order and pay 1,500,000 yen in compensation. The court based its decision on job unsuitability and union-busting. It did not find the family suffering caused by *tanshinfunin* in itself sufficient reason to bar companies from transferring their employees, although it did acknowledge the adverse effects of *tanshinfunin* on family life. Two months previous to the Higuchi decision, the Osaka Supreme Court found against the plaintiff in a *tanshinfunin* case, *Yoshida v. Towa Paint,* on the grounds that Towa Paint had legitimate business reasons for transferring Mr. Yoshida, and that the family inconveniences caused by his transfer were at a level one would normally expect an employee to bear. Thus the courts have not set a clear precedent for the abolishing of forced *tanshinfunin* practice.

For an extensive discussion of these cases, refer to the Muneto et al. (1986) and Miyaji articles (1986).

4. The Equal Employment Opportunity Law, effective in April 1986, stipulates that companies must "endeavor" to give women and men equal opportunity and treatment in job assignments and promotion. In response, many companies that had previously not given women the chance to enter the management track opened it to women, under the condition that they agreed to accept any transfer. Those who did not want to commit themselves in advance to transfer had to accept the dead-end, general office track. Most women choose against the management track because they do not want to give up their chances to marry and have families, and personnel officers try to convince them that the two cannot be reconciled (Miyaji 1986:38–48).

5. For a fascinating fictional account of the struggles of one daughter-in-law to manage the caretaking of her elderly father-in-law while simultaneously keeping her job, see Sawako Ariyoshi's *The Twilight Years* (1984).

6. On a return trip to Japan in 1988, I learned that the company had changed this policy to accommodate those who wish to retire between ages of fifty-five and sixty. In the new policy, both sexes may retire between these ages without penalty in retirement benefits.

7. According to the Labor Ministry, in 1965, 49.3 percent of women workers retired at pregnancy or childbirth; by 1981, the figure had dropped to 21.7 percent, indicating the trend toward continuing employment throughout the childbearing years (*Rōdōshō Fujin Kyoku* 1985:90, appendix).

## 4  Time Off

1. Lebra (1976:136) defines *tatemae* as "the standard, principle, or rule by which one is bound, at least outwardly." *Tatemae* is usually contrasted with *honne,* "one's natural, real, or inner wishes or proclivities."

2. The recent boom in "culture centers," where housewives can attend classes in any number of subjects from language to cooking to flower design,

is an example of this; another is the availability of in-company training classes for both blue- and white-collar (especially male) employees throughout their careers (Rohlen 1992). Yet another example is the "Silver Talent Centers" program, a contract-work system established by the government for retirees. The purpose of the program is not only to give senior citizens opportunities to earn extra income but also to get them out into the community and give them meaning in life through work. There are many training programs sponsored by Silver Centers, yet the training is not meant to be merely instrumental—i.e., to enable the worker to perform a new job—but also intrinsically worthwhile, as a kind of study. Those who graduate from a training program but cannot find work in the skill, I am told, do not consider their time wasted, but rather value the opportunity to have learned something new (personal correspondence with Dr. Hajime Saito, executive member of the Tokyo Metropolitan Senior Citizen's Work Promotion Foundation).

3. Tadashi Hanami (in Krauss et al., 1984:113–114) elaborates on the nature of the employer/employee relationship as follows: "The ideal relationship between employees and employers in Japan is akin to the traditional one among family members. No notion of rights or obligations in the Western sense has developed. The employee/employer relationship . . . lacks clearly defined obligations and rights. . . . The abstractness and vagueness of Japanese contracts is based on the presumption that the parties to the contract have, or will have, a close personal relationship and can rely on mutual understanding and trust."

4. *Enryoshite* means to "do *enryo*," to feel restraint about putting one's self-interests first, above the group. The ability to exert self-restraint is a sign of empathy for others and, hence, maturity. In this case, one could not go home quickly or easily, but had to take great care to apologize to the proper authorities and to one's coworkers before leaving.

5. Most of the respondents were married (83.9 percent), with long years of service (43.15 percent had over fifteen years; 37.4 percent, five to ten years). Eighty percent had children: their ages ranged from 19 and under (0.1 percent), to 20–29 (11.4 percent), 30–34 (21.5 percent), 35–39 (25.9 percent), 40–44 (22.4 percent), 45–49 (10.3 percent), 50–54 (2.0 percent), and over 60 (0.3 percent). Most were office workers (51.1 percent) or professionally skilled (32.4 percent). Only 6 percent were in skilled production. The industries that employed them were service (22.3 percent), government (39.5 percent), manufacturing (12.2 percent), communications/transport (8.6 percent), sales (7.7 percent), construction (2.1 percent), electric, gas, and water (0.6 percent), forestry (0.2 percent), and fisheries (0.1 percent). The survey's main purpose was to discover the effects on women's health of the introduction of microelectronics into the workplace.

## 5 Enjoying Azumi: Building Careers

1. A *shokutaku* is an employee whose status is between that of *paato* and regular employee. Her benefits are greater than those of a *paato* but not as extensive as those of regulars. In many firms, employees (usually male) are kept on after retirement as *shokutaku,* in unranked jobs at fractions of their former salaries.

2. The Labor Standards Law of 1947 provided women workers the right to take twelve weeks of maternity leave: six before birth and six afterward. Women who had children age one and under were given *ikuji jikan* ("child-care time"), one-half hour twice daily for breast-feeding and so on. Azumi's union made an arrangement with the company whereby the child-care time would be taken for one hour a day at the end of the day, and could be taken for up to the first two years after birth. Since the promulgation of the Equal Employment Opportunity Act, the maternity leave has been extended to six weeks prepartum and eight weeks postpartum, with six weeks of the postpartum period compulsory (Miyaji 1986:27).

3. She also remarked at another point in the interview that the fact that she was having difficulties balancing home and work duties contributed to her desire to step down from being *hanchō.*

4. This was in violation of the Labor Standards Law.

5. Nakada san was not the only middle-aged employee I knew who wished to find a partner. Taniguchi san (forty-eight) was still hoping, and so was Matsumura *hanchō* (thirty-six). Murakami *kakarichō* (forty) also said she had not had the luck to find a spouse but should not be treated as different from other women because of it. To the Japanese, marriage is not only considered to be a natural step in the process of life, it is also essential to being recognized as, and becoming, a mature adult (see Lebra 1984:78). The next step is having children—how often my coworkers urged me to have a baby! Without one, I was excluded from the conversations on child care, and in their eyes I had not yet fulfilled my duty to my mother—how happy she would be, they told me, if I would have a baby!

## 6 Social Life

1. The word used here is *gō.* It carries implications of karma, or fate. Shimizu san, who is a member of a new religion, the Soka Gakkai, may have been referring to the Buddhist notion of *gōsho,* or "karmic hindrances." According to Hardacre (1984:197), some Japanese believe that women face greater obstacles than men in achieving salvation, and that this is women's *gōsho.* Unfortunately, I did not have an opportunity to discuss this further with Shimizu san.

2. According to Bestor (1989:206) the term *tsukiai,* aside from its meaning of "obligatory personal relationships" as defined by Reiko Atsumi (1979), also

"implies a sense of calculating personal advantage . . . that may come from establishing or maintaining a particular relationship." In my interactions with female coworkers at Azumi, *tsukiai* were conceived of as obligatory, especially when they were formal, company-sponsored after-hours meetings or events. They were instrumental in the sense that getting together was promoted by management as a means to smoothing personal relationships for a better functioning of the workplace. Informal *tsukiai,* such as regular gatherings of women during work breaks, or weekend parties that women themselves organized on occasion for their self-selected groups, were much more for pure enjoyment and mutual interest, which Atsumi characterizes as a facet of friendship.

3. The exceptions are the men who enter in mid-career, who are not in the track for their age cohort nor in that of young men who entered the year they did. Such men are at a loss for gauging their relative positions in the company.

## 7 Improving the Workplace: Channels for Grievances

1. In 1987 *Zensen Dōmei* dissolved and joined with the *Jidōsha Sōren* (Confederation of Japan Automobile Workers' Unions), *Denki Rōren* (Japanese Federation of Electrical Machine Workers' Unions), and fifty-one other industrial federations to form *Rengō*, the Japanese Private Sector Trade Union Confederation.

2. *Wa* has many meanings. Used alone it also means "peace"; another usage is (mathematical) "sum." Used along with other characters, it can also signify "Japan" or "Japanese," as in *washoku,* Japanese food. For an analysis of the significance of *wa* in the Japanese workplace, see Rohlen, *For Harmony and Strength* (University of California Press 1974). For an application to baseball, see Whiting, *You Gotta Have Wa* (Macmillan Co. 1989).

3. With the promulgation of the Equal Employment Opportunity Act in 1986, the Labor Standards Law was amended to provide all women this two-week extension in maternity leave, for a total of six weeks before birth and eight afterward.

## 8 Budgeting and Day Care

1. It is common in Japan for unmarried daughters to live at home until marriage. In fact, those few who did not were the subject of much disapproval and gossip at the factory. If a young woman did not live at home, people surmised there must be something wrong in her relationship with her parents, and she must have some flaw in her character. People also thought a young woman living alone would be lonely and vulnerable to advances by men.

2. For a fascinating account of the history of Japan's day-care system see Kathleen Uno's 1987 doctoral dissertation from the University of California at Berkeley, "Day Care and Family Life in Industrializing Japan." For additional information in English on preschools and kindergartens in Japan, see

Sarane Spence Boocock, 1989, "Controlled Diversity: An Overview of the Japanese Preschool System" in *Journal of Japanese Studies,* 15:1.

3. *Paasonaru* (Jan. 1, 1988:47) states that in 1987, 1.3 percent of all spaces in licensed centers were reserved for infants of less than one year old; 15.7 percent were reserved for children ages one to two. After two years of age, the capacity widens greatly, making it easy to register a child.

4. *Paasonaru* (Jan. 1, 1988:44) attributes this lengthening of public and private licensed centers to the uproar over dangerous conditions in "baby hotels," to which parents without other options resorted. It reports that the "baby hotels" issue was even debated in the Diet in 1981.

5. Fujii san paid 12,600 yen a month for her five-year-old and 37,400 yen a month for her one-year-old. The day care amounted to about one-half of her 110,000 yen take-home pay.

6. In fact, Fujii san once admitted that she thought day-care instructors could teach her child better than she, since they were professionals and each had her own area of interest and expertise.

## 9 Juggling Home and Work

1. For a portrait of a farming woman in contemporary rural Japan, see Gail Bernstein's *Haruko's World* (1983). R. J. Smith and Ella Wiswell provide a detailed account of the lives of rural women in the early Showa period in *The Women of Suyemura* (1982). Both books show women contributing a good deal of hard work to their households.

2. In 1986, 19.4 percent of all women workers, some 4,520,000, were engaged as family workers (National Institute of Employment and Vocational Research, 1988:102).

3. Japanese washing machines are rarely the fully automatic, large-capacity machines used in the United States, but are smaller, semi- or nonautomatic machines. It is necessary for most households to do several loads every night.

4. She was taking child-care time. Women with children under age one have the legal right to take off one-half hour a day, twice daily, for child care. At Azumi women took child-care time in a one-hour lump at the day's end.

5. *Pachinko* are vertical "pinball" machines played in smoke-filled game rooms very like slot-machine casinos in atmosphere, having gaudy lights and high noise levels. It is considered more of a men's than a women's pastime. *Pachinko* parlors are also thought to be associated with organized crime.

6. She did not want people to think that her children had a bad mother. *Pachinko* parlors are considered slightly disreputable for women; at least, it would not be socially acceptable for a mother to leave her children at home in the evening in order to go and play a game at the corner parlor. Their reputation may have improved because of Takako Doi, former head of the Japan Socialist party, who is an aficionado of the game.

# References Cited

Ariyoshi, Sawako. 1984. *The Twilight Years*. Tokyo: Kodansha.

Atsumi, Reiko. 1979. "Tsukiai—Obligatory Human Relationships of Japanese White-Collar Employees." *Human Organization* 38, no. 1: 63–70.

Bernstein, Gail. 1983. *Haruko's World*. Stanford, Calif.: Stanford University Press.

Bestor, Theodore. 1989. *Neighborhood Tokyo*. Stanford: Stanford University Press.

Boocock, Sarane. 1989. "Controlled Diversity: An Overview of the Japanese Preschool System." *Journal of Japanese Studies* 15, no. 1: 41–65.

Brinton, Mary. 1993. *Women and the Economic Miracle: Gender and Work in Postwar Japan*. Berkeley: University of California Press.

Clark, Rodney. 1979. *The Japanese Company*. New Haven and London: Yale University Press.

Cole, Robert. 1971. *Japanese Blue Collar*. Berkeley and Los Angeles: University of California Press.

Cook, Alice, and Hiroko Hayashi. 1980. *Working Women in Japan: Discrimination, Resistance and Reform*. Ithaca, N.Y.: Cornell University Press.

Edwards, Walter. 1987. "The Commercialized Wedding as Ritual: A Window on Social Values." *Journal of Japanese Studies* 13, no. 1 (1987): 51–78.

Fujin Kyōiku Kenkyūkai. 1987. *Tōkei ni Miru Josei no Genjō*. Tokyo: Shuppan Kabushiki Gaisha.

Fujita, Mariko. 1989. "It's All Mother's Fault: Childcare and the Socialization of Working Mothers in Japan." *Journal of Japanese Studies* 15, no. 1 (1989): 67–91.

Fuse, Akiko. 1982. "Rōdōsha Kazoku no Seikatsu." In Toshio Kurokawa et al., eds., *Gendai no Fujin Rōdō*. Vol. 3: *Rōdōsha no Seikatsu to Kaji, Ikuji*. Tokyo: Rōdōjunpōsha.

190                                                        References Cited

Hakuhodo Institute for Life and Living, ed. 1983. *Hitonami: Keeping Up with the Satos.* Tokyo: Hakuhodo Institute for Life and Living.

———. 1984. *Japanese Women in Turmoil.* Tokyo: Hakuhodo Institute for Life and Living.

Hanami, Tadashi. 1984. "Conflict in Industrial Relations and Labor Law." In Ellis Krauss, Thomas Rohlen, and Patricia Steinhoff, eds., *Conflict in Japan.* Honolulu: University of Hawaii Press.

———. 1985. *Labour Law and Industrial Relations in Japan.* Deventer, The Netherlands: Klewer Law and Taxation Publishers.

———. 1987. *Koyō to Rōdō* [Employment and labor]. Tokyo: NHK Shimin Daigaku.

Hardacre, Helen. 1984. *Lay Buddhism in Contemporary Japan.* Princeton, N.J.: Princeton University Press.

Hasegawa, Michiko. 1984. "Equal Opportunity Legislation Is Unnecessary." *Japan Echo* 11, no. 4, pp. 55–58.

Hashimoto, Hiroko. 1982. "Fujin Rōdōsha to Hoiku Mondai." In Toshio Kurokawa et al., eds. *Rōdōsha no Seikatsu to Kaji, Ikuji.* Tokyo: Rōdō-junpōsha.

Hoiku Hakusho Henshū Iinkai. 1983. *Hoiku Hakusho.* Tokyo: Sōdō Bunka.

Hoikuen o Kangaeru Hahaoya no Kai. 1984. *Hoikuen 110 Ban.* Tokyo: Yukkusha.

Honda, Junryō. 1985. "Onna no Sengo Shi: Danjo Koyō Byōdō Hō: Josei Hogo to Danjo Byōdō o Hakari ni Kakete. . . ." *Asahi Journal,* vol. 27, no. 10, pp. 75–80.

———.1986. "Kijun Hō de Shokuba wa Ima." Publication from the Osaka Shūritsu Daigaku Symposium, October 4, 1986.

Imamura, Anne. 1987. *Urban Japanese Housewife: At Home and in the Community.* Honolulu: University of Hawaii Press.

Ishida, Eiko. 1988. "Konwaku suru Josei Rōdō to Hoiku no Shōhinka." In *Rōdō Undō Kenkyū* 6, no. 224 (1988): 8–11.

Iwao, Sumiko. 1993. *The Japanese Woman: Traditional Image and Changing Reality.* New York: The Free Press.

Kanter, Rosabeth Moss. 1977. *Men and Women of the Corporation.* New York: Basic Books.

Keizai Kikaku chō. 1989. *Keizai Hakusho.* Tokyo: Ōkurashō.

Koike, Kazuo. 1987. "Human Resource Development and Labor-Management Relations." In Kozo Yamamura and Yasukichi Yasuba, eds., *The Political Economy of Japan,* vol. 1: *The Domestic Transformation,* 289–330.

Kondo, Dorinne. 1982. "Work, Family and the Self: A Cultural Analysis of Japanese Family Enterprise." Ph.D. dissertation, Harvard University.

———. 1990. *Crafting Selves: Power, Gender, and Discourses of Identity in a Japanese Workplace.* Chicago: University of Chicago Press.

Kuda, Megumi, and N. Matsubara. 1988. "Hoikuen o Tetteiteki ni Erabu." *Paasonaru,* no. 68 (January 1988): 43–52.

Lebra, Takie S. 1976. *Japanese Patterns of Behavior.* Honolulu: University of Hawaii Press.

———. 1981. "Japanese Women in Male Dominant Careers." *Ethnology* 20 (4):291–306.

———. 1984a. *Japanese Women.* Honolulu: University of Hawaii Press.

———. 1984b. "Nonconfrontational Strategies for Management of Interpersonal Conflicts." In Ellis Krauss, Thomas Rohlen, and Patricia Steinhoff, eds., *Conflict in Japan.* Honolulu: University of Hawaii Press.

———. 1992. "Gender and Culture in Japanese Political Economy: Self-Portrayals of Prominent Businesswomen." In Shumpei Kumon and Henry Rosovsky, eds., *The Political Economy of Japan,* vol. 3, Cultural and Social Dynamics. Stanford: Stanford University Press.

Lock, Margaret. 1980. *East Asian Medicine in Urban Japan.* Berkeley and Los Angeles: University of California Press.

Mclendon, James. 1983. "The Office: Way Station or Blind Alley?" In David Plath, ed., *Work and Lifecourse in Japan.* Albany: SUNY Press.

Miyaji, Mitsuko, Taiji Muneto, Fujiwara, and Maekawa. 1986. " 'Ningenrashisa' o Tsuikyūshita Saiban: Asahi Kasai Kaijō Hoken Jiken Kobe Chisai Hanketsu no Igi." *Rōdōhōritsu Junpō,* no. 1154 (October 1986).

Miyaji, Mitsuko. 1986a. "Tanshin Funin ni 'Isharyoka Hanketsu' o Kachitotta Zensonpō Asahi Kasai/Higuchi Jiken no Tatakai." In *Minshu Hōritsu,* no. 195 (November 1986).

Miyaji, Mitsuko, and Junryo Honda. 1986b. *Onna no Rōdō Kijunhō.* Tokyo: Rōdōjunpōsha.

Moore, Sally Falk. 1977. *Law as Process.* London: Routledge and Kegan Paul.

Mouer, Ross, and Yoshio Sugimoto. 1986. *Images of Japanese Society.* London: KPI.

National Institute of Employment and Vocational Research. 1988. *Women Workers in Japan.* Tokyo: NIEVR.

OECD. 1985. *The Integration of Women into the Economy.* Paris: OECD.

———. 1987. *Employment Outlook.* Paris: OECD.

———. 1988. *Human Resources and Corporate Strategy.* Paris: OECD.

Parkinson, Lorraine. 1989. "Japan's Equal Employment Opportunity Law: An Alternative Approach to Social Change." *Columbia Law Review* 89, no. 3 (April 1989): 604–661.

Pharr, Susan. 1990. *Losing Face: Status Politics in Japan.* Berkeley and Los Angeles: University of California Press.

Rōdōshō, eds. 1989. *Rōdō Hakusho.* Tokyo: Rōdōshō.

Rōdōshō Fujin Kyoku, eds. 1985, 1987, 1988, 1992. *Fujin Rōdō no Jitsujō.* Tokyo: Rōdōshō Fujin Kyoku.

Rohlen, Thomas. 1974. *For Harmony and Strength.* Berkeley and Los Angeles: University of California Press.

———. 1992. "Learning: The Mobilization of Knowledge in the Japanese Political-Economy." In Henry Rosovsky, ed. *The Political Economy of Japan,* vol. 3, Cultural and Social Dynamics. Stanford, Calif.: Stanford University Press.

Salamon, Sandra. 1975. "Male Chauvinism as a Manifestation of Love in Marriage." In David Plath, ed. *Adult Episodes in Japan.* Leiden: E. J. Brill.

Saito, Shigeo. 1982. *Tsumatachi no Shishūki.* Tokyo: Kyodo Tsushinsha.

Sakamoto, Fukuko. 1989. "Kintōhō Seiritsu Go no Josei Rōdōsha no Jōkyō." *Zenki,* vol. 9, no. 579, pp. 90–101.

Shin Nihon Fujin no Kai. 1985. *Hataraku Fujin no Shigoto to Kenkō, Bosei.* Tokyo: Shin Nihon Fujin no Kai.

Shinotsuka, Eiko. 1982. *Nihon no Joshi Rōdō.* Tokyo: Tōyō Keizai Shinpō Sha.

Shirai, Taishiro. 1983. "A Theory of Enterprise Unionism." In Taishiro Shirai, ed. *Contemporary Industrial Relations in Japan.* Madison: University of Wisconsin Press.

Sievers, Sharon. 1981. "Feminist Criticism in Japan Politics in the 1880s: The Experience of Kishida Toshiko." *Signs,* vol. 6, no. 4, 602–616.

Simpson, Diane L. 1985. "Women in Japan's Struggle for Labor Reform." In Norbert Soldon, ed., *The World of Women's Trade Unionism.* Westport, Conn.: Greenwood Press.

Sklar, Kathryn. 1973. *Catherine Beecher: A Study in American Domesticity.* New York: W. W. Norton.

Smith, Robert J., and E. Wiswell. 1982. *The Women of Suyemura.* Chicago: University of Chicago Press.

———. 1987. "Persistent Ideological and Structural Bases for Gender Inequality in Contemporary Japan." *Journal of Japanese Studies,* vol. 12, no. 2.

Sōmuchō Tōkei Kyoku, eds. 1985. *Rōdōryoku Chōsa Nenpō Shōwa 59.* Tokyo: Management and Coordination Agency, Bureau of Statistics.

———. 1988. *Nihon Tōkei Nenkan.* Tokyo: Management and Coordination Agency, Bureau of Statistics.

Takenaka, Emiko. 1989. *Sengo Joshi Rōdō Shiron.* Tokyo: Yuhikaku.

Tsuya, Noriko. 1990. "Kodomo o Umu Umanai wa Kojin no Sentaku." *Ekonomisuto* 8, no. 7 (1990): 348–351.

Ueno, Chizuko. 1987a. "Genesis of the Urban Housewife." *Japan Quarterly* 34, no. 2 (April–June).

———. 1987b. "The Position of Japanese Women Reconsidered." *Current Anthropology* 28, no. 4 (August–October).

Uno, Kathleen S. 1987. "Day Care and Family Life in Industrializing Japan." Ph.D dissertation, University of California at Berkeley.

Upham, Frank. 1987. *Law and Social Change in Postwar Japan.* Cambridge, Mass.: Harvard University Press.

Vogel, Ezra. 1963. *Japan's New Middle Class.* Berkeley and Los Angeles: University of California Press.

Vogel, Suzanne. 1978. "The Professional Housewife." In Merry White and Barbara Maloney, eds., *Proceedings of the Tokyo Symposium on Women,* 150–155. Tokyo: International Group for the Study of Women.

Wagatsuma, Hiroshi, and A. Rossett. 1986. "The Implications of Apology: Law and Culture in Japan and the U.S." *Law and Society Review,* vol. 20, no. 4, pp. 461–498.

Westwood, Sally. 1984. *All Day, Every Day.* Urbana: University of Illinois Press.

White, Merry. 1987. *The Japanese Educational Challenge: A Commitment to Children.* New York: The Free Press.

Whiting, Robert. 1989. *You Gotta Have Wa.* New York: Macmillan.

*The World Almanac and Book of Facts.* 1988. New York: Pharos Books.

# Index

absence: apology for, 74–76; rate, 86; and work flow, 116
age: and interpersonal relations, 114–116; and job mobility, 55; limits in recruiting, 34
aging: and job tenure, 63, 66–68; as a management problem, 68–73, 175; and personal relations, 113–116
alcohol, consumption of, 44, 106–107
allowance, for rank, 92, 133
arranged marriage, 95
attendance ratings, 76. *See also* absence

bonus, 117, 118
Brinton, Mary, 176
*buchō,* 12

carpal tunnel syndrome, 65, 137
child care, and kin support, 99, 101
child care time *(ikuji jikan),* 97, 100, 134
child rearing, husband's participation in, 156–160
children's attitude toward mother working, 162–163
classification of workers, 12
cliques, 110–111
Cole, Robert, 53, 62, 110–111

commitment to the firm, 3
complaints. *See* conflict management
conflict management, 78, 121, 126, 139
conformity, 85
Confucian values: and moral exhortations, 113; and work attitudes, 80
consensus, 85
consumption patterns, 140–144; attitudes toward, 27–28, 153
Cook, Alice, 58, 63
cooperation among groups, 116–117

defiance, of directives, 44, 45
discipline, and work regulations, 43
Doi *kachō,* 31, 117, 118, 140, 165
day care: after school, 147; attitudes toward, 148–151; center at Azumi, 130; conditions for admission to, 146; fees, 147; history of, 145–148; survey at Azumi, 148

Edwards, Walter, 22, 155
education, children's and mothers' responsibilities, 59–60
equal opportunity in employment, 171–173
Equal Opportunity in Employment Act (EEOA), 3, 173–175; and job